RESEARCH PAPERS
A New Guide

Samuel Draper
SUNY Rockland Community College

KENDALL/HUNT PUBLISHING COMPANY
4050 Westmark Drive Dubuque, Iowa 52002

Dedication

For Janet Gluckman
My extraordinary student, gifted writer, and courageous woman.

Cover photograph by Samuel Draper of James Marina, top left; Kenneth Lynch, top right; and Ann Marie Keenan, lower left; of the Mentor/Talented Student Honors Program, Rockland Community College, SUNY, Suffern, NY

Libarary of Congress Catalog Card Number: 86–83232

ISBN 0–8403–6675–2

Printed in the United States of America
10 9 8 7 6

Contents

Preface

RESEARCH PAPERS: A NEW GUIDE

MLA and APA Styles and Formats has been written expressly for several audiences, the first involving the students in English 910, the Research Paper Workshop, recommended for all Rockland Community College students who plan to transfer to a four-year college, the second involving any college student, who, without the benefit of a research paper class, is willing to study this guide and master its contents. English 910 is based on the concept that any student can be taught the essential techniques of the research paper in ten sessions of approximately an hour each, exclusive of the time required to accomplish the research itself and to write the research paper. Since those ten sessions can be accomplished handily in a six-week time period, English 910 has been established as a six-week module for one credit of English. It has been the practice of the English 910 instructors at RCC to require students to submit their outlines and rough drafts to be read by the teachers in the presence of the researchers before the final typing of the paper is accomplished. Such a procedure is advantageous at once to the student and the teacher. After the typing of the paper, the student presents the original paper to the professor for whom he is originally writing the paper and a xerox copy to the English 910 instructor. This arrangement involves a "two-for-one" or "two-fer" idea, two grades satisfied by one paper, and was prompted by the assignment of research papers in all RCC honors courses which make up the Mentor/Talented Student Honors Program. Obviously, English 910 serves these students well, for they transfer to some of the country's most prestigious colleges where the research essay is held in high regard.

For other students, not in honor courses nor in classes where research essays are assigned, who wish to learn the MLA and APA styles and formats, they may enroll in English 910 on a Pass/Fail basis; for a Pass grade, such students attend all sessions of the workshop, complete homework assignments on research form and on proper methods of preparing the Works Cited (MLA) or References (APA), both terms referring to bibliographic entries.

Finally, students who do not take the English 910 class may learn the essentials of proper research techniques by reading, studying or even by consulting this Research Papers: A New Guide.

Furthermore, the research paper is one of the most widely used and highly respected academic tools. Expository in purpose, the research paper explores a problem, analyzes and interprets an idea or answers one or more questions. It uses many sources which must be collected and evaluated and then presented with organization and precision to provide an interesting and original learning experience, both to the writer of the paper and to the reader. Many prestigious universities, including Harvard and the University of California, explain in their respective style sheets for research writing, that a research paper, properly researched and written, may involve the most valuable of all learning experiences in college.

Acknowledgments

First, I wish to thank the Sabbatical Leave Committee of the Academic Senate of Rockland Community College, SUNY, which recommended my proposal, Research Papers: A New Guide, as worthy of a sabbatical grant for the summer of 1984. I wish also to thank Dr. F. Thomas Clark, President of Rockland Community College, for granting the final approval of my Sabbatical Leave with its implicit trust and financial assistance.

Especial thanks go to Prof. Libby Bay, chairperson of English, and coordinator of the Mentor/Talented Student Honors Program along with the writer of this Guide. Early in 1977, she and I decided that research papers would be assigned in all honors courses at RCC, with the exception of Honors Calculus, a judgment which has been met with approval by many prestigious senior institutions to which our MTS Honors graduates regularly transfer as juniors.

The author is certainly grateful to Olive Tamborelle, a reference librarian at St. Thomas Aquinas College, Sparkhill, NY, for having researched the section on General Reference Works with such intelligence and diligence. Suzanne Weekly, formerly of the RCC Library, and now head of the St. Thomas Aquinas Library, should also be singled out for her many years of assisting our researchers and for her professionalism in regard to research materials. Now the responsibility of "guided tours" for the English 910 students of our library resources has fallen on Grace Patterson of the RCC Library Reference Staff. Also the author wishes to thank Elsie Ciabattoni of the RCC Library for her assistance.

All professors who are mentors and honors professors in the MTS Honors Program should be acknowledged: Professors David Beisel, Phyllis Krasnow, Andrew Breidenbach, Libby Bay, Ann Fey, Dan Masterson, John Allman, Neal Kreitzer, Nancy Hazelton, James Thelen, Joseph Gusmano, Maurice Guild, J. Matthew Pirone, Thomas Fitzpatrick, Fred Gross, Sue Schulman, Wilma Frank, David Kurzman, Gregory Julian, and Beverly Brown. Their admirable mentoring, splendid teaching and adherence to the philosophy of academic excellence are exemplary—and inspirational.

I wish to thank all my colleagues, too, at Empire State College for their support of the academic research paper and this volume, particularly Diane Worby and Rhoda Miller who assist me with the research paper sessions offered by ESC both in Rockland and Orange Counties.

I acknowledge my appreciation to Peggie Flynn, an MTS Honors Program assistant, and English Department secretary, and Edna Eckhouse, an English Department secretary, for their wholehearted cooperation on this project and on many others. And their lively charm and enthusiasm are appreciated by all of us. Finally, I acknowledge my gratitude and debt to Kimberly Pfaff, Patrice Kerins, two excellent undergraduates, whose research papers enhance this Guide; and Linda Reda who prepared the manuscript.

—S. D.

Mentor/Talented Student Honors Program, Liberal Arts and Sciences,
Rockland Community College,
State University of New York,
Suffern, NY 10901

FIRST SESSION

MLA (Modern Language Association) Style Guide

The research paper consists of:

1. The Writer's Own Words

   As the writer of the paper you can express your own ideas in your own words and NO DOCUMENTATION IS NECESSARY. Sometimes this writing is referred to as the student's own words. The introduction and conclusion of the research paper are written in the student's own words, for example. (Later on, more information will be given as to when it is appropriate to include some of your own thoughts in the research essay).

Here is an example of an introduction to a literature paper in the student's own words.

The changing beliefs, new ideas, and advancements in artistic achievements of the twentieth century have produced a powerful experimental movement affecting all aspects of the creative arts. The artist has probed into new, perhaps more meaningful techniques of expression. Literature, in particular, has been the object of many innovative forces. As a result, writers have expanded their literature into new art forms. Two of these new art forms concern what is referred to as the "Experimental Novel" or "Anti-Novel" and the "Literature of the Absurd." The aim of this paper is to demonstrate that Auto-da-Fe (1936), a novel by Elias Canetti (1905–), is a splendid example of the recent trends in literature which reflect characteristics of both the "Anti-Novel" and "Literature of the Absurd."

2. Short, Integrated Quotations

   These quotations by someone else other than the writer of the paper are LESS THAN FOUR LINES OF TYPING (from the left margin to the right margin of the rough draft); they are INTEGRATED DIRECTLY INTO THE DOUBLE-SPACING OF THE PAPER ITSELF. QUOTATION MARKS ARE NEEDED, BUT THE TRADITIONAL FOOTNOTE TO INDICATE THE SOURCE OF THE QUOTATION IS NO LONGER USED. THE NAME OF THE PERSON WHO IS BEING QUOTED IS GIVEN AND THE PAGE NUMBER OF THE SOURCE WHERE THE QUOTATION APPEARS IS ALSO USED. THESE INNOVATIVE ADDITIONS REPLACE THE TRADITIONAL FOOTNOTE IN THE TEXT OF THE RESEARCH PAPER.

Here are examples of short, integrated quotations:

One authority asserts that "sign language includes all forms of codification in which words, numbers, and punctuation signs have been supplemented by gestures. . ." (Knapp 20). NOTICE THAT FOOTNOTES ARE NO LONGER USED TO IDENTIFY A SHORT QUOTATION. When you do not use the authority's name to introduce the material, include his or her name within parentheses along with a specific page number of the source from which the quotation is taken. IN OTHER WORDS, THE AUTHOR'S NAME AND THE PAGE NUMBER REPLACE THE TRADITIONAL FOOTNOTE. You can find the reference to Knapp's book Nonverbal Communication in Human Interaction listed at the back of the research paper text in the section called "Works Cited," a new term which replaces the traditional term "Bibliography."

Another method of documenting the short, integrated quotation is as follows:

Mark L. Knapp (20) asserts that "sign language includes all forms of codification in which words, numbers, and punctuation signs have been supplemented by gestures. . . ."

3. Long Quotations

   These quotations by someone other than the writer of the paper are MORE THAN FOUR LINES OF TYPING (from the left margin to the right margin of the rough draft); LONG QUOTATIONS ARE NO LONGER BLOCK-INDENTED AND SINGLE-SPACED. THE LONG QUOTATION SHOULD BE DOUBLE-SPACED AND SEPARATED FROM THE TEXT BY TRIPLE-SPACING. The long quotation should be properly introduced by using a colon to link the quotation to its introduction. QUOTATION MARKS ARE NOT NEEDED FOR THE LONG QUOTATION EXCEPT FOR QUOTATIONS WITHIN THE QUOTATION. INDENT THE QUOTATION TEN SPACES FROM THE REGULAR MARGIN; HOWEVER, THE RIGHT MARGIN NEEDS NO SPECIAL INDENTATION.

Example of the long quotation is shown below:

In Yoknapatawpha Country, Cleanth Brooks, an authority on Faulkner, praises Rosa Millard:

> Miss Rosa is another of Faulkner's Puritans . . . she has not much concern for ritual and devotion . . . she believes powerfully in good words; and she believes in God's justice. . . . To her, goodness means the nurturing and fostering of children, mercy for the helpless, aid for the poor . . . . (95)

Period goes before the parenthesis in a long quotation.

Had the original long quotation begun with a paragraph indentation, then the words "Miss Rosa" would have been indented 15 spaces from the left margin.

4. Paraphrase

   Paraphrase is the use or borrowing of SOMEBODY ELSE'S MATERIAL, IDEAS, OPINIONS, THOUGHTS, OR INTERPRETATIONS WHICH YOU (the writer of the paper) PUT INTO YOUR OWN WORDS. Repeat: YOUR OWN WORDS. You must change the style and vocabulary of the original writing you are paraphrasing. THE TRADITIONAL FOOTNOTE IS NO LONGER REQUIRED, BUT YOU MUST INCLUDE IN THE PARAPHRASE THE NAME OF THE PERSON WHOSE WORK IS BEING PARAPHRASED AND THE PAGE NUMBER OF THE WORK BEING PARAPHRASED.

An example of paraphrase follows:

Mark Schorer writes (15–16) that Lawrence incorporated his own life experiences rather than dry, hypothetical case studies in Sons and Lovers. This novel reflects Lawrence's own relationship with his mother, a closeness referred to often by psychologists as the Freudian Oedipal concept. The novel spells out the enormous influence a mother can have on her son's psycho-sexual development and how the son may become emotionally warped from such maternal domination. The novel was perhaps the first fictional treatment in the 20th century to present psychological data as a means of comprehending human behavior. When the novel was published in 1913, when the Lawrences had left England for Bavaria, the reviews of the novel were good, but few realized how influential this work was to become in English literature.

Or you might document the paraphrase in this manner:

One eminent literary critic explains that Lawrence incorporated his own life experiences rather than dry, hypothetical case studies in Sons and Lovers. This novel reflects Lawrence's own relationship with his mother, a closeness referred to often by psychologists as the Freudian Oedipal concept .... but few realized how influential this work was to become in English literature (Schorer 15–16).

Original material on Sons and Lovers by Mark Schorer which was paraphrased above, in the student's own style and vocabulary, is as follows:

On May 29, 1913, after the Lawrences had gone back to Bavaria, Sons and Lovers was published. There were some good reviews but the sale of the book was small. Nothing suggested that D. H. Lawrence had written one of the great English novels. We should remind ourselves of the historical importance of this novel. It was perhaps the first work of twentieth-century fiction to impress many readers with the availability of modern psychological theory as a means of understanding human relationships. Founded, as the novel is, on that soon most familiar of Freudian patterns, the so-called Oedipus complex, we can hardly estimate the ultimate if not the immediate impact of a work that in 1913 declared so clearly that a mother could be almost demonically determined to possess her son's will, or that a son's sexual character could be so corrupted by that possession. Lawrence's treatment remains compelling today, however, because his was not a theoretical use of this situation, but an experienced human dilemma, his own.*

THE AUTHORITY'S OR CRITIC'S NAME SHOULD BE INTRODUCED INTO AND USED CONSISTENTLY THROUGHOUT THE PAPER

In writing the research paper, you can choose one of two ways to cite your source: first, you introduce every short quotation you use, every long quotation you include, and every paraphrase you compose with the name of the authority or critic whose work is being quoted or paraphrased.

*Mark Schorer, D. H. Lawrence. New York: Dell, 1968, 15–16.

For example: According to Isaiah Berlin, distinguished Oxford philosopher, "Tolstoy's philosophy of history has, on the whole, not obtained the attention which it deserves, whether as an intrinsically interesting view or as an occurrence in the history of ideas, or even as an element . . . in Tolstoy himself" (4). If you can identify the source accurately, you should do so. If you cannot identify the critic or authority, do not identify him or her as "author." In that case, you should simply omit the identification. Second, you can simply put the authority's name in parentheses after the quotation or paraphrase.

If there is no human authority to cite, use the name of the SOURCE ITSELF. Example: The New York Times explained this week that "video and audio have been rubbing elbows for some time, and last year, with the advent of hi-fi video cassette recorders, relations between the two were getting very close." (9 Sept. 1984, sec. 2: 1+).

USE DIFFERENT TYPES OF INTRODUCTIONS OF CRITICS' AND AUTHORITIES' NAMES, IN DIFFERENT POSITIONS IN YOUR SENTENCES FOR THE SAKE OF FLUENT, FLEXIBLE WRITING

"Eveline's inertia," Clive Hart, an authority on Joyce, interprets, "is revealed by the excessive value she places in the routine satisfactions of her present existence . . ." (50). (Notice that the critic's name Clive Hart is introduced into the second element of the sentence, not the first. If you use the critic's or authority's name first in the sentence, this practice becomes monotonous. In other words do not write each introduction with: Lionel Trilling finds . . . , etc. Eric Bentley believes . . . ; Marjorie Hope Nicolson asserts. . . .

Another example of using the critic's name in the second element of the sentence:

"When Stevenson was a young boy," continues James Pope-Hennessy, a British literary critic, "he frequently suffered from nightmares in which he was leading a double life. In his dreams he worked during the day in a horrid surgery" (17).

An example of using the critic's name in the third or last element of the sentence:

"Mr. Hyde is an embodiment of the savage aggressive id who slumbers in us all," concludes Albert Guerard, an authority on the psychological "double" (9).

Another example:

Others believe an opposite point of view (Bentley 34 and Valency 21).

In introducing the short quotation, the long quotation, and the paraphrase, you should not only vary the position of the authority's name but also vary the verbs you use so that you do not continue to write the cliché, "Professor Mark Schorer says." Rather you should use synonyms for the verb "says." For example, Professor Libby Bay suggests, Professor Joseph Gusmano asserts, Professor Joseph Pirone declares, Professor Dan Masterson continues, etc.

OTHER VERBS WHICH WILL PROVIDE VARIETY ARE: point out, conclude, argue, posit, interpret, analyze, write, report, reveal, affirm, contend, explain, think, declare, mention, state, verify, confirm, continue, insist, believe, speculate, conjecture, assert.

EXPLORING SOME RELATIONSHIPS CONCERNING SHORT QUOTATIONS, PARAPHRASE, LONG QUOTATIONS, AND THE STUDENT WRITER'S OWN WORDS

Have you ever thought of how much you should involve yourself and your own ideas in the research paper? How much paraphrase should you write? How many short integrated quotations should you include? How many long quotations? THE FIGURES GIVEN HERE MAY AID YOU IN ANSWERING THESE QUESTIONS ALTHOUGH THESE PERCENTAGES ARE NOT TO BE TAKEN LITERALLY: THEY REPRESENT POSSIBLE SUGGESTIONS FOR ASSISTANCE. NOBODY WILL EVER SUBJECT YOUR RESEARCH PAPER TO THIS KIND OF PERCENTAGE ANALYSIS. THE THREE DIFFERENT KINDS OF RESEARCH PAPERS EXPLORING VARIOUS RELATIONSHIPS CONCERNING SHORT QUOTATIONS, PARAPHRASE, LONG QUOTATIONS, AND THE STUDENT WRITER'S OWN WORDS (Research Paper I, II, and III) ARE MEANT TO BE HELPFUL, HOWEVER, NOT RESTRICTING OR CONFINING.

Research Paper I

6% The student writer's own words	(Introduction of the paper, perhaps, transition sentences, conclusion, etc.)
42% Short integrated quotations	
42% Paraphrase	
10% Long quotations	(Long quotations should be used very sparingly and only with good cause, for most readers simply skip them.)

The student receives an assignment to research a particular idea and to write a research paper based ALMOST ENTIRELY ON THE SOURCES OF OTHERS, or the student, on his own, may wish to research a given topic and write a paper without involving his own ideas, reactions, or interpretations. In this kind of paper, the student's own ideas would not be relevant or correct. Examples: "Jonathan Swift: What His Contemporaries Thought of Him and His Literature," is a paper that has sometimes been assigned in an eighteenth-century English literature class. "The Quarrel of The Cid: Corneille and The French Academy," is another example of this kind of essay which the writer of this Guide submitted, in a French course at UCLA, as a paper which included no ideas of the student writer himself.

Research Paper II

15% The student writer's own words
35% Short integrated quotations
35% Paraphrase
15% Long quotations

The student writer wishes to use some of his own ideas in combination with the opinions of others. Many research papers on literature fall into this category owing to the interpretive nature of such papers. See the student research paper on "War and Peace" at the end of this guide in which the student gives some of her own ideas about the subject.

Research Paper III

50% The student writer's own words

20% Short integrated quotations

20% Paraphrase

10% Long quotations

The student writer has become somewhat of an expert in his/her own field and in the thesis which is nothing more than an advanced research paper. The B.A., M.A., or Ph.D. thesis might be considered a research paper of category III, in which the student relies more on his own ideas, opinions, and interpretations than he relies on the sources of others.

SECOND SESSION

Work on Paraphrase

Paraphrase is the borrowing of—or use of—somebody else's material, ideas, opinions, thoughts, or interpretations which you (the writer of the paper) will rewrite into your own words—in approximately the same number of words as the original. You should change the style and vocabulary of the original material as much as possible. DO NOT SLAVISHLY TRANSLATE WORD FOR WORD FROM THE ORIGINAL INTO YOUR OWN VOCABULARY. OFTEN STRONG PARAPHRASES INCORPORATE THE SAME IDEAS AS THE ORIGINAL SOURCE BUT IN A DIFFERENT SEQUENCE.

Sometimes you will have to use a word which appears in the original because no accurate synonym can be found. For example, if the original piece contains the word "ratiocination" or "synchronicity," both psychological terms; or "comprehensive market analysis," a business or economics term; or "romanticism," "classicism," or "naturalism," literary ideas; or any other technical term from any specific field of learning, you may use these words in the paraphrase without violating the integrity of the paraphrase.

Some authorities suggest that whenever you must use any of these technical words (for which there are no accurate one-word synonyms), the technical words should be enclosed in quotation marks. The only difficulty with such an idea is that words put in quotation marks call attention to themselves, and if there are too many words in the paraphrase, its effectiveness is reduced. The readers pay too much attention to the words in quotation marks rather than to the thoughts of the paraphrase.

Since footnotes are no longer used in the text of the research paper to indicate the sources of short and long quotations and paraphrases, you must indicate the source of the paraphrase by including the name of the authority or critic whose work you are paraphrasing EITHER IN THE TEXT ITSELF OR IN PARENTHESES AT THE APPROPRIATE PLACE IN THE SENTENCE.

For example,

> According to Mark Slonim, an authority on Russian literature, Russian literature did not make its appearance in the Western world until the second half of the nineteenth century, when Europe and America first heard of Turgenev, Tolstoy, Dostoevsky, and Gogol (3).

Or

> One authority on Russian literature (Mark Slonim 3) asserts that Russian literature came on the scene, in terms of Western culture, during the last half of the nineteenth century. . . .

Remember also that the page number, arabic numerals, without the traditional "p." for "page" is given inside the parentheses. The reader of the paraphrase can locate the original material from which the paraphrase was made by looking at the back of the text of the paper itself under "Works Cited" (formerly referred to as "Bibliography") and locate the book alphabetically, according to the author's last name, Slonim, Mark. An Outline of Russian Literature.

ORIGINAL PIECE ON JOHANN WOLFGANG VON GOETHE

Johann Wolfgang von Goethe (1749–1832) is not only the chief literary figure of Germany but one of the greatest writers of all time. He applied his genius to almost all forms of literature, including the drama, for which, in spite of his experience as the director of the court theatre of Weimar, he had only a wayward talent. He never developed a sure grasp of dramatic composition, and if he had developed it, he would in all probability have quickly relinquished it in order to launch into philosophical discussions or to indulge his supreme talent for poetry. Nor were correctives at hand in the feeble German theatre to turn Goethe into an accomplished playwright. If, nevertheless, his contributions to the theatre were far from negligible, and if one of his plays, Faust, is the outstanding dramatic work of the romantic movement, the reason lies in his singular power of self-expression and in his happy choice of subjects. Faust's insatiable thirst for experience, for example, epitomizes European romanticism. It is with good reason that the venturesomeness of Western man in all fields of human activity and his insatiable desire for self realization have been called "Faustian."*

ACCEPTABLE PARAPHRASE OF THE ABOVE MATERIAL DONE BY A STUDENT

Johann Wolfgang von Goethe (1749–1832)† author of the play Faust (Part I, 1808; Part II, 1832)† never became a master playwright despite his term of office as director of the court theatre at Weimar. The then impoverished German theatre could offer little to Goethe as a budding playwright in order that he might perfect himself as a masterful dramatist. Faust, nevertheless stands for and summarizes European romanticism because Faust's unending search for life's experiences is universal in Western mankind who continues to explore all areas of human accomplishment. Indeed, Faust's prolonged search for self-reliance and self-actualization or "self-realization" has come to be known as "Faustian." In any case, if Goethe had learned his dramatic craft to greater advantage, he, in all likelihood, would have abandoned it for philosophy or poetry for which he had prodigious gifts (Gassner 504).

Or

John Gassner (504), an authority on world drama and a Yale professor, explains that Johann Wolfgang von Goethe (1749–1832)† author of the play Faust (Part I, 1808; Part II, 1832)† never became a master playwright despite his term of office as director of the court theatre at Weimar, etc., etc.

Or

John Gassner, an authority on world drama, writes in A Treasury of the Theatre (504) that Johann Wolfgang von Goethe (1749–1832)† author of the play Faust, etc., etc.

*From John Gassner. "Introduction: Johann Wolfgang von Goethe." A Treasury of the Theatre.

†The birth and death dates of all the important figures mentioned in the research paper should be given in parentheses after the figure's name when first introduced. Likewise, the publication date of all important works should be included in parentheses after the title of the work.

ORIGINAL PIECE ON D. H. LAWRENCE'S SONS AND LOVERS

On May 29, 1913, after the Lawrences had gone back to Bavaria, Sons and Lovers was published. There were some good reviews but the sale of the book was small. Nothing suggested that D. H. Lawrence had written one of the great English novels. We should remind ourselves of the historical importance of this novel. It was perhaps the first work of twentieth-century fiction to impress many readers with the availability of modern psychological theory as a means of understanding human relationships. Founded, as the novel is, on that soon most familiar of Freudian patterns, the so-called Oedipus complex, we can hardly estimate the ultimate if not the immediate impact of a work that in 1913 declared so clearly that a mother could be almost demonically determined to possess her son's will, or that a son's sexual character could be so corrupted by that possession. Lawrence's treatment remains compelling today, however, because his was not a theoretical use of this situation, but an experienced human dilemma, his own.*

ACCEPTABLE PARAPHRASE OF THE LAWRENCE MATERIAL ABOVE DONE BY A STUDENT

One expert on D. H. Lawrence contends that Lawrence personally suffered from Freud's Oedipus complex, which then became source material for his novel Sons and Lovers (Schorer 15–16). The Oedipal pattern suggests that the mother's and son's strong attachment to each other may eventually have negative results, particularly for the son. This presentation of a psychological theory manifested, as it was, in a work of fiction introduced many readers to the then new theories of modern psychology. Historically, Lawrence's book was most important, for it was one of the first creative works to show the psychological aspects of human relationships. However, the buying public did not recognize this idea. Since its publication in 1913, after the Lawrences had left England and gone back to Bavaria, recognition has grown until today Sons and Lovers is considered one of the great English novels.

ANOTHER STUDENT PARAPHRASE OF THE SAME LAWRENCE MATERIAL

When originally published, Sons and Lovers (1913) by D. H. Lawrence (1885–1930), was the first piece of twentieth-century fiction to indicate the connection between modern psychological theory and its significance in understanding inter-personal relationships, contends Mark Schorer, an authority on Lawrence. The number of books sold at the time of publication was unimpressive, however. Based on what is now an almost household acquaintance with the so-called Oedipus complex, it is difficult to assess the influence since publication of a work which so clearly indicates how in the warped relationship between mother and son, the latter's sexual development and character could be maimed. Lawrence's thesis remains, even in modern times, arresting, because it is based, not on fantasy, fiction, or theory, but on an actual—his own—human predicament (15–16).

*Mark Schorer, D. H. Lawrence. New York: Dell, 1968, 15–16.

Paraphrase One of the Passages Below for Practice

Alfred Adler was born in a Vienna suburb, February 7, 1870, the second son of a Jewish merchant who originated from a German-speaking part of Hungary. As a child Adler got along well with the other children in the neighborhood and he always considered himself a real Viennese, which indeed he was, from being able to speak the dialect to singing Wienerlieder (Viennese songs) and songs by Schubert. Adler graduated from medical school in Vienna in 1895 and after military service established himself as a practitioner in a modest neighborhood. It was in 1902 that Adler, together with three others, was invited by Freud to meet every Wednesday in Freud's house to discuss problems of neurosis. It was this small discussion circle which eventually grew into the Vienna Psychoanalytic Society. Adler became its president in 1910 but resigned from it a year later.*

FOR PRACTICING PARAPHRASE

. . . I believe that our future salvation lies in a movement away from sexual polarization and the prison of gender toward a world in which individual roles and the modes of personal behavior can be freely chosen. The ideal toward which I believe we should move is best described by the term "androgyny." This ancient Greek word—from andro (male) and gyn (female)—defines a condition under which the characteristics of the sexes and the human impulses expressed by men and women, are not rigidly assigned. Androgyny seeks to liberate the individual from the confines of the appropriate. . . . Androgyny suggests a spirit of reconciliation between the sexes; it suggests, further, a full range of experience open to individuals who may, as women, be aggressive, as men tender; it suggests a spectrum upon which human beings choose their places without regard to propriety or custom.†

FOR PRACTICING PARAPHRASE

Although Eliot referred to Yeats as "the greatest poet" of his time, Eliot was himself the most famous. A man of keen intellect, capable of developing a philosophical position as well as a new rhythm and intonation, trained in classics, fluent in French and German, Eliot was better equipped than any other poet to bring verse fully into the twentieth century. As James Joyce remarked of him in a notebook, T. S. Eliot abolished the idea of poetry for ladies. In discrediting many of his predecessors, in choosing with the utmost fastidiousness what he needed and wanted from the literary tradition in several languages, Eliot gave modern literature one of its most distinctive idioms. When The Waste Land was published in 1922, it gave Eliot his central position in modern poetry. No one has been able to encompass so much material with so much dexterity, or to express the ennui and the horror of so many aspects of the modern world. Though the poem was made up of fragments, they were like pieces of a jigsaw puzzle which might be joined if certain spiritual conditions were met. In this way,

*Heinz L. Ansbacher, "Goal-Oriented Individual Psychology: Alfred Adler's Theory," in Operational Theories of Personality, ed. Arthur Burton. New York: Brunner/Mazel, 1974, 101.

†Carolyn G. Heilbrun. "Introduction," Toward a Recognition of Androgyny, New York: Knopf, 1973, ix–x.

Eliot's attitude towards fragmentation was different from Pound's—Eliot saw a necessity for recomposing the world, while Pound thought it might remain in fragments and still have a paradisal aspect which the poet could elicit. In other words, Pound accepted discontinuity as the only way in which the world could be regarded, while Eliot rejected it and looked for a seamless world. Eliot began to find it in Christianity. . . . His last important poems, The Four Quartets, constitute the achievement of his spiritual quest.*

NOTE: IF YOU LIKE TO SUBSTITUTE YOUR OWN MATERIAL TO PARAPHRASE (BUSINESS, ECONOMICS, PHILOSOPHY, HISTORY, SOCIOLOGY, PSYCHOLOGY AND/OR OTHERS), PLEASE DO SO. THE ESSENTIAL THING IS THAT YOU PRACTICE PARAPHRASING MATERIAL WHICH IS COLLEGE MATERIAL, NOT SIMPLISTIC NEWSPAPER ARTICLES FROM THE TABLOID NEWSPAPERS, FOR EXAMPLE. IF YOU PREFER TO CHOOSE YOUR OWN MATERIAL TO PARAPHRASE, BE SURE TO COPY THE ORIGINAL MATERIAL AND HAND IT TO YOUR INSTRUCTOR ALONG WITH THE PARAPHRASE EXERCISE. YOUR INSTRUCTOR WILL NEED THE ORIGINAL SOURCES IN ORDER TO COMPARE YOUR PARAPHRASE WITH THE ORIGINAL.

*From Richard Ellmann and Robert O'Clair. The Norton Anthology of Modern Poetry. Copyright © 1973 by W. W. Norton and Company, Inc., etc. Reprinted with permission.

THIRD SESSION

Combining Short Quotations and Paraphrase

Since you will want to use SHORT QUOTATIONS in your paper, PARAPHRASE, an occasional LONG QUOTATION, as well as some of YOUR OWN WORDS if appropriate to your topic, you should learn to COMBINE SHORT QUOTATIONS AND PARAPHRASE within the same paragraph. Learning this COMBINATION TECHNIQUE is indispensable if you wish to demonstrate excellence in your paper.

ORIGINAL MATERIAL TO BE COMBINED INTO SHORT QUOTATIONS AND PARAPHRASE

In T. S. Eliot's Murder in the Cathedral, the Archbishop Becket utters a sentence which suggests that people cannot stand very much reality. The sad dictum may serve to summarize the purport of The Wild Duck by Henrik Ibsen (1828–1906). And the play goes on to suggest that it is wicked for one person to seek to impose upon another a greater amount of reality than can comfortably be borne. That this should be the "message" of a play of Henrik Ibsen came as a great surprise—indeed, a shock—when The Wild Duck was first presented in 1884.

And even now it is likely to startle any reader or playgoer acquainted with the author's characteristic early work. For Ibsen was an outstanding figure in the movement of modern art and intellect that subjected all existing institutions, and the conventions of thought and feeling, to relentless scrutiny in the interests of truth; it was the stern judgment of this movement that society is a contrivance to mask or evade or distort reality. The effort to discriminate between what is real and what is illusory is of course not a new endeavor for literature. But in the modern epoch it has been undertaken with a new particularity and aggressiveness, and by none more than by Ibsen. He had made his reputation with four plays—Pillars of Society (1877), A Doll's House (1879), Ghosts (1881) and An Enemy of the People (1882)—and in each of them he had pressed home the view that falsehood, whether in the form of social lies and hypocrisy or of self-deception, weakens the fabric of life and deprives human kind of its dignity. Expectably enough, his work had met with resistance by the larger part of his audience, that is to say, the more conventional part. But by the same token, the "advanced" minority, a growing force in European culture, received him as a master of truth. In his lifetime and for many years after his death, people spoke of "Ibsenism," by which they meant the radical questioning of all established and respectable modes of life and the unyielding opposition to sham and pretense. It can therefore be imagined with what bewilderment and dismay the Ibsenites received a play which said that truth may be dangerous to life, that not every man is worthy to tell it or receive it, and that the avoidance and concealment of the truth, or even a lie, may have a vital beneficence.*

STUDENT EXAMPLE OF THE COMBINATION EXERCISE USING THE MATERIAL ON IBSEN PRINTED ABOVE

Henrik Ibsen (1828–1906) had become famous for four of his dramas Pillars of Society (1877), A Doll's House (1879), Ghosts (1881), and An Enemy of the People (1882), contends Lionel Trilling, a major literary critic. These plays assert that truth was deemed to be preferable to prevarications, falsehoods, duplicities, and deceits, for such lies tend to destroy social structures. In these four specifics, Ibsen is seen to be the champion of truth, a crusader for what is real as opposed to what is imaginary (201). "Expectably enough," the authority adds, "his work had met with resistance by the larger part of his audience, that is to say, the more conventional part. By the same token, the 'advanced' minority . . . received him as a master of truth" (Trilling 201). However, when The Wild Duck (1884) was first seen on the stage, Trilling explains, the audience was shocked at its contents which suggest that humankind cannot withstand the pressures of too much reality or truth. The play further elaborates on the idea that it is sinful or heartless for one individual human being to force upon another a greater dose of truth than one can swallow (201). "It can therefore be imagined with what bewilderment and dismay the Ibsenites received a play which said that truth may be dangerous to life," Trilling further posits, ". . . and the avoidance and concealment of truth or a lie, may have a vital beneficence" (202). The same idea, that truth may be dangerous, is spoken by the Archbishop Becket in T. S. Eliot's Murder in the Cathedral, and that concept does symbolize the main theme of The Wild Duck (201). When people spoke of "Ibsenism" in Ibsen's lifetime and even many years after his demise . . . "they meant the radical questioning of all established and respectable modes of life and the unyielding opposition to sham and pretense" (Trilling 202).

The student combined short, integrated quotations with paraphrase, approximately half and half. The student writer made the paraphrases more than one sentence, correct procedure whenever possible. The student was likewise correct in using short quotations as long as possible, without exceeding the maximum of four lines of typing on the rough draft.

SINCE APPROPRIATE DOCUMENTATION FOR EACH SHORT, INTEGRATED QUOTATION AND EACH PARAPHRASE IS REQUIRED, AND SINCE THE TRADITIONAL FOOTNOTES ARE NO LONGER USED IN THE TEXT OF THE RESEARCH PAPER ITSELF TO INDICATE SOURCES, THE NEW METHODOLOGY IS AS FOLLOWS:

Indicate the source of the quotation by using the name of the critic or authority in the short, integrated quotations or in the paraphrase, as well as the page number on which the material occurs which is being quoted or paraphrased. Since Lionel Trilling, a distinguished literary critic, is the author of the original piece printed above, notice how the student used Trilling's name and the pages 201 and 202 (the pages of the original Trilling source) throughout the combination exercise which combines both short quotations and paraphrase.

ORIGINAL MATERIAL TO BE COMBINED INTO SHORT QUOTATIONS AND PARAPHRASE

On the literary side, Edith Wharton (1862–1937) was almost without peer in her American generation as a judge of achievements in fiction and poetry. She was decades ahead of critical opinion in her high assessment and appreciation of poets as remote from each other as John Donne and Walt Whitman; and her most unfashionable pronouncements in the 1920s on new literary idols like Joyce and Eliot seem, in certain special perspectives, to have more cogency with every passing year.

Her dedication to her own creative task, meanwhile, was complete, and no one worked more strenuously or revised more thoroughly. It was her habit of deprecating her talent—when measured against that of the great masters of fiction—that could be construed by the unperceptive as indicating a less than wholehearted involvement. It is the conviction behind this biography, after the statutory observation that her work was decidedly uneven, that a good many of her books have survived (to pick up her word) and will continue to survive. They have an elegant shapeliness of form. . . . With their muted subtleties, their preciseness of allusion, and above all the compassion for the wounded or thwarted life that flows through them, they are among the handsomest achievement in our literature. I have wondered, with other admirers of Edith Wharton, whether her reputation might today stand even higher if she had been a man. Her writings . . . are also quiet, a continuing testimony to the female experience under modern historical and social conditions, to the modes of entrapment, betrayal, and exclusion devised for women in the first decades of the American and European twentieth century.*

FURTHER ORIGINAL MATERIAL TO BE COMBINED INTO SHORT QUOTATIONS AND PARAPHRASE

Ethan Frome (1911) by Edith Wharton (1863–1937) . . . was in good part the product of her personal life during the previous few agitated years. Into no earlier work of fiction, not even The House of Mirth (1905), had she poured such deep and intense private emotions. Ethan Frome in this regard was a major turning point, whether or not it was also the very finest of her literary achievements. Edith had hitherto reserved her strongest feelings for poetry; henceforth, they would go into her novels and stories.

The treatment both of seeing and character shows Edith Wharton in perfect command of the methods of literary realism; in its grim and unrelenting way, Ethan Frome is a classic of the realistic genre. At the same time, it is Edith Wharton's most effectively American work; her felt affinities with the American literary tradition were never more evident. A certain Melvillian grandeur went into the configuration of her tragically conceived hero. Despite her early disclaimers, the spirit of Nathaniel Hawthorne pervades the New England landscape of the novella and lies behind the moral desolation of Ethan Frome—a desolation as complete in its special manner as that of his namesake, Hawthorne's Ethan Brand.

But the great and durable vitality of the tale comes at last from the personal feelings Edith Wharton invested in it, the feelings by which she lived her narrative. Ethan Frome portrays her personal situation, as she had come to appraise it, carried to a far extreme, transplanted to a remote rural scene, and rendered utterly hopeless by circumstance.†

(For the purposes of identification, R. W. B. Lewis is a well-known critic of American Literature and a Professor of English at Yale.)

*From EDITH WHARTON: A Biography, by R. W. B. Lewis.

†Ibid.

FURTHER ORIGINAL MATERIAL TO BE COMBINED INTO SHORT QUOTATIONS AND PARAPHRASE

What was the credo of the intellectuals during these years of revolt (World War I: 1914–1918)? Not many of them accepted all the propositions in the following rough summary; yet it suggests, perhaps, the general drift of their collective opinion:

They believed in a greater degree of sex freedom than had been permitted by the strict American code; and as for the discussion of sex, not only did they believe it should be free, but some of them appeared to believe it should be continuous. . . . From the early days of the decade (1920), when they thrilled at the lackadaisical petting of F. Scott Fitzgerald's young thinkers and at the boldness of Edna St. Vincent Millay's announcement that her candle burned at both ends and could not last the night, to the latter days when they were all agog over the literature of homosexuality and went by the thousands to take Eugene O'Neill's five-hour lesson in psychopathology, Strange Interlude, they read about sex, talked about sex, thought about sex, and defied anybody to say No.

In particular, they defied the enforcement of propriety by legislation and detested all the influences to which they attributed it. They hated the Methodist lobby, John S. Sumner, and all defenders of censorship; they pictured the Puritan, even of Colonial days, as a blue-nosed, cracked-voiced hypocrite; and they looked at Victorianism as half indecent and half funny. . . .

Most of them were passionate anti-prohibitionists, and this fact, together with their dislike of censorship and their skepticism about political and social regeneration, made them dubious about all reform movements and distrustful of all reformers. They emphatically did not believe that they were their brothers' keepers; anybody who did not regard tolerance as one of the supreme virtues was to them intolerable. . . .

They were mostly, though not all, religious skeptics. If there was less shouting agnosticism and atheism in the nineteen-twenties than in the eighteen-nineties, it was chiefly because disbelief was no longer considered sensational and because irreligious intellectuals, feeling no evangelical urge to make over others in their own image, were content quietly to stay away from church. . . .

They were united in a scorn of the great bourgeois majority which they held responsible for prohibition, censorship, Fundamentalism, and other repressions. They emulated Mencken in their disgust at Babbits, Rotarians, the Ku-Klux Klan, Service-with-a-Smile, boosters, and supersalesmen.*

NOTE: IF YOU WOULD LIKE TO SUBSTITUTE YOUR OWN MATERIAL (FROM ANY COLLEGE FIELD OF STUDY), WHICH MAY APPEAL TO YOU MORE THAN THE EXAMPLES HERE, PLEASE DO SO. JUST REMEMBER THAT IN ORDER TO ACCOMPLISH THE EXERCISE OF COMBINING SHORT, INTEGRATED QUOTATIONS AND PARAPHRASE WITHIN THE SAME PARAGRAPHS, YOU WILL HAVE TO PROVIDE YOUR INSTRUCTOR WITH A COPY OF THE ORIGINAL MATERIAL YOU PLAN TO USE FOR THE COMBINATION EXERCISE.

STUDENTS OF LITERATURE SHOULD ALSO BE AWARE THAT SHORT AND LONG PLAYS, SHORT STORIES, NOVELLAS, AND NOVELS ARE ALSO TO BE USED AS SOURCES FROM WHICH ONE COMBINES SHORT, INTEGRATED QUOTATIONS AND PARAPHRASE AS WELL AS THE STUDENT'S OWN REACTIONS TO THE FICTION ITSELF. THE STUDENT'S OWN INTERPRETATIONS IN THE STUDENT'S OWN WORDS ARE USUALLY APPROPRIATE WHEN WRITING ABOUT LITERATURE, AN INTERPRETIVE ART.

ORIGINAL WORDS FROM SISTER CARRIE. A NOVEL, BY THEODORE DREISER TO BE COMBINED INTO SHORT, INTEGRATED QUOTATIONS AND PARAPHRASE AND SOME OF THE STUDENT'S OWN IDEAS IF THE STUDENT IS SO INCLINED

By January he [Hurstwood] had about concluded that the game was up with him. Life had always seemed a precious thing, but now constant want and weakened vitality had made the charms of earth rather dull and inconspicuous. Several times, when fortune pressed most harshly, he thought he would end his troubles; but with a change of weather, or the arrival of a quarter or a dime, his mood would change, and he would wait. . . . He was beginning to find, in his wretched clothing and meagre state of body, that people took him for a chronic type of bum and beggar. Police hustled him along, restaurant and lodging-house keepers turned him out promptly the moment he had his due; pedestrians waved him off. He found it more and more difficult to get anything from anybody. . . .

One day, in the middle of the winter, the sharpest spell of the season set in. It broke grey and cold in the first day, and on the second snowed. Poor luck pursuing him, he had secured but ten cents by nightfall, and this he had spent for food. At evening he found himself at the Boulevard [Broadway] and Sixty-seventh Street, where he finally turned his face Boweryward. Especially fatigued because of the wandering propensity which had seized him in the morning, he now half dragged his wet feet, shuffling the soles upon the sidewalk. An old, thin coat was turned up about his red ears—his cracked derby hat was pulled down until it turned them outward. His hands were in his pockets.*

STUDENT EXAMPLE OF THE COMBINATION IN WHICH THE STUDENT HAS NOT ONLY COMBINED SHORT, INTEGRATED QUOTATIONS WITH PARAPHRASE BUT ALSO HAS INCLUDED SOME OF HIS/HER OWN IDEAS

(Note: If you are a student of literature, it is a good practice to get in the habit of not only combining short, integrated quotations and paraphrase, but also including some of your own thoughts about the ideas at hand).

Some research paper topics do not lend themselves to the inclusions of the student's own ideas and interpretations; for example, a paper dealing with the social structure of the French Court at the height of the reign of King Louis XIV would not allow for the student's own ideas in this historical research essay, for these ideas would be intrusive and not at all appropriate. SEE THE LAST SECTION OF THE FIRST SESSION FOR MORE EXPLANATIONS OF WHEN IT IS APPROPRIATE OR NOT FOR YOU TO INCLUDE SOME OF YOUR OWN IDEAS.

*From Theodore Dreiser, Sister Carrie: A Norton Critical Edition. Copyright © 1970 by W. W. Norton and Company, Inc. Reprinted with permission.

A STUDENT'S HANDLING OF THE MATERIAL FROM SISTER CARRIE

When Sister Carrie begins to work regularly in the New York theatre, she moves from poorer quarters to more expensive ones, and Hurstwood is simply left alone to fend for himself on the streets of New York. In January he had about decided that the experience of life had just about come to an end (S.C. 360). "Life had always seemed a precious thing, but now constant want and weakened vitality had made the charms of earth rather dull and inconspicuous" (S.C. 360). It is obvious to the reader that Hurstwood has thought about suicide, for he has very little to live for now that Carrie has deserted him. One also realizes that Carrie, although she may appear to some as cruel-hearted in abandoning the man she formerly lived with, must be about her own business, her own career of making it to the top where she will never be in want. It was true that Hurstwood had postponed taking his own life when the weather changed from bad to good or he would be given a dime or quarter for a night's lodgings (S.C. 360). "He was beginning to find, in his wretched clothing and meagre state of body, that people took him for a chronic type of bum and beggar. Police hustled him along, restaurant and lodging-house keepers turned him out promptly the moment he had his due" (S.C. 360). On one day, in the middle of January, the cruelest weather broke forth, occurring bleak and sharp the first day, and on the second, it snowed. Bad luck was hounding him, so that he had only received ten cents as a panhandler by dark. He bought some food with this money. . . . He faced the direction of the Bowery (S.C. 361). ". . . He now half dragged his wet feet, shuffling the soles upon the sidewalk. An old, thin coat was turned up about his red ears—his cracked derby hat was pulled down until it turned outward. His hands were in his pockets" (S.C. 361). Indeed, he started realizing that in his rag-tag clothes and thin body, people would consider him a derelict, a down-and-out drifter or castaway (S.C. 360). On the winter day when Hurstwood felt shunned and was penniless, Dreiser reminds the reader that tears came into Hurstwood's eyes.

If the student's literature research paper dealt with a thesis concerning Dreiser's "naturalism" and the thesis incorproated the demonstration of these "ideas of naturalism" in two novels of Theodore Dreiser, not only Sister Carrie but also Jennie Gerhardt, the student would indicate paraphrase and quotations from Jennie Gerhardt in the same manner as he or she had with Sister Carrie, that is, by abbreviating the title Jennie Gerhardt as J.G. within the parentheses along with the appropriate page number from Jennie Gerhard, i.e., (J.G. 123). WHEN STUDENTS ARE WRITING A RESEARCH PAPER BASED ON ONE OR MORE PRIMARY SOURCES, SUCH AS ANY SHORT PLAY, LONG PLAY, SHORT STORIES, NOVELLAS, AND NOVELS, OR ANY ORIGINAL WORK such as BEING AND NOTHINGNESS BY SARTRE, OR REALMS OF THE HUMAN UNCONSCIOUS BY GROF, OR THE ARCHETYPES AND THE COLLECTIVE UNCONSCIOUS BY JUNG, THESE WORKS ARE CONSIDERED PRIMARY SOURCES. WHEN QUOTING OR PARAPHRASING THESE ORIGINAL PRIMARY SOURCES, ALWAYS ABBREVIATE THE TITLES OF THESE WORKS WITHIN THE PARENTHESES—ALONG WITH THE CORRECT PAGE INDICATING THE SOURCE OF THE QUOTATION OR PARAPHRASE. SEE EXAMPLES ABOVE USING SISTER CARRIE, A NOVEL, A PRIMARY SOURCE BY DREISER.

ABBREVIATIONS OF THE TITLES OF PRIMARY SOURCES ARE USED WHEN THE RESEARCH PAPER IS INVOLVED WITH ONE OR MORE PRIMARY SOURCES WHICH ARE CONSTANTLY BEING QUOTED AND PARAPHRASED. IF YOU REFERRED ONLY ONCE IN A PAPER TO JUNG'S THE ARCHETYPES AND THE COLLECTIVE UNCONSCIOUS, THIS QUOTATION, FOR EXAMPLE, WOULD BE HANDLED IN THIS MANNER:

According to Carl Gustave Jung, writing in The Archetypes and the Unconscious, ".." (102).

or Carl Gustave Jung explains: ".." (Archetypes and the Unconcious 102).

WHEN YOU QUOTE OR PARAPHRASE SECONDARY SOURCES (TEXTBOOKS, ARTICLES AND CRITICISM, ENCYCLOPEDIAS, NEWSPAPERS, LECTURES ABOUT PRIMARY SOURCES, ETC.) BY QUOTING AND PARAPHRASING THESE SECONDARY SOURCES, DO NOT ABBREVIATE THE TITLES OF THESE SECONDARY SOURCES WITHIN THE PARENTHESES. THE PAGE NUMBER FROM THE SECONDARY SOURCE IS SUFFICIENT AS LONG AS THE SOURCE IS INDICATED IN THE TEXT OF THE PAPER OR WITHIN THE PARENTHESES. ABBREVIATIONS OF TITLES ARE USED WITHIN THE PARENTHESES WHEN A PAPER IS BASED ONLY ON ONE OR MORE PRIMARY SOURCES WHICH WILL CONSTANTLY BE QUOTED AND PARAPHRASED.

***NOTE: ABBREVIATIONS FOR ALL PRIMARY SOURCES such as Sister Carrie, a novel, may be done as follows: (SC 123), rather than (S.C. 123), or Jennie Gerhardt as (JG 110), rather than (J.G. 110).

DISTINCTIONS BETWEEN PRIMARY AND SECONDARY SOURCES

Field	Primary Sources	Secondary Sources
Literature	Novels, plays, short stories, poems, novellas, autobiographies, letters, diaries	magazine and journal articles, biographies, textbooks on literature, critical books on writers and literature
Social Sciences	case studies, findings from surveys and from questionnaires, reports of social workers, psychiatrists, and laboratory technicians	textbooks on the social sciences, evaluations in reports, documents, magazine and journal articles
Political Science Government History	The Congressional Record, speeches by politicians, speeches by presidents, writings of presidents, and other government officers, reports of agencies and departments	magazine and journal articles, newspaper articles and reports, political journals and newsletters, and all textbooks on history, politics, etc.

DISTINCTIONS BETWEEN PRIMARY AND SECONDARY SOURCES—*Continued*

Field	Primary Sources	Secondary Sources
Sciences	experiments of all kinds done in the laboratory, findings from tests and experiments, observations, discoveries, and test patterns, tools and methods of testing	textbooks on all fields of science, interpretations and discussions of test data as found in magazines and journals, newspaper articles about science
Fine Arts (music, painting, sculpture and other arts)	paintings, musical compositions, films, sculptures, reproductions of all kinds	textbooks on all the fine arts, magazine and journal articles, biographies, and critical works about artists and their work
Business	market research and testing, technical studies and investigations, drawings, designs, models, memoranda and letters, computer research, computer data	textbooks on all parts of business, magazine and journal articles, critical reviews, government documents
Education	term projects, pilot studies, tests and test data, surveys, interviews, statistics, computer data	textbooks on education, magazines and journals on education, analyses of educational experiments

FOURTH SESSION

Research in the College Library

PART ONE

A BRIEF GUIDE TO THE LIBRARY OF CONGRESS CLASSIFICATION SYSTEM BOOKS

A GENERAL WORKS
- AE Encyclopedias (general)
- AG Handbooks
- AM Museums
- AP Periodicals (general)
- AS Learned institutions
- AY Almanacs

B PHILOSOPHY, RELIGION
- BC Logic
- BF Psychology
- BL-BR Religion
- BS Bible

C AUXILIARY SCIENCES OF HISTORY
- CC Archeology
- CR Heraldry
- CG Genealogy
- CT Biography

D HISTORY: GENERAL & OLD WORLD
- DA Great Britain
- DC France
- DD Germany
- DF Greece
- DK Russia
- DP Spain, Portugal
- DT Africa

E HISTORY: AMERICA (U.S. GENERAL)
- E 11–99 Indians
- E 184 U.S. Foreign population
- E 185 Negroes
- E 186 (U.S. history by period)
- E 186–199 U.S. Hist.–Colonial period
- E 201–298 U.S. Hist.–Revolution
- E 456–655 U.S. Hist.–Civil War
- E 740–839 U.S. Hist.–20th Century
- E 784–805 U.S. Hist.–1919–1933
- E 806–812 U.S. Hist.–1933–1945
- E 813– U.S. Hist.–1945–

F HISTORY: AMERICA
- F 116–130 New York State
- F 1001–1035 Canada
- F 1203–1409 Mexico
- F 1434–1545 Central America
- F 1601–2151 West Indies
- F 2201–3799 South America

G GEOGRAPHY, ANTHROPOLOGY, RECREATION
- GB Physical geography
- GN Anthropology
- GR Folklore
- GY Sports
- GV 187–547 Physical Education
- GV 1580–1799 Dancing (Dance)

H SOCIAL SCIENCES
- HA Statistics (general)
- HB Economics
- HC Industry. Natural resources
- HD Economic policy. Industry
- HE Communication. Transportation
- HF Commerce
- HF 5601–5689 Accounting
- HJ 2005–2199 U.S. Budget
- HM–HV Sociology
- HQ Family
- HQ 750–799 Children (development)
- HQ 1101–2030 Woman
- HT 815–1445 Slavery
- HV (Social work) Social Service
- HV 1–4630 Poverty
- HV 2350–2990 Deaf
- HV 5001–5720 Alcoholism
- HV 5725–5770 Smoking
- HV 5800–5840 Narcotic habit
- HV 6001–9920 Crime & criminals
- HX 1–55 Socialism
- HX 626–795 Communism

J POLITICAL SCIENCE
- J–JQ Constitutional Law
- JK U.S. Politics & government
- JK International Law

K LAW

L EDUCATION
- LA Education–History
- LB 1043–1044 Audio-visual education
- LB 1050–1632 Reading & Teaching
- LB 2801–2997 School management
- LC 1041–7 Vocational education
- LC 3951–3990 Exceptional children

M MUSIC
- M 1–2199 (Scores)
- ML Musicology
- MT Music-instruction & study

N FINE ARTS
- NA Architecture
- NB Sculpture
- NC Drawing
- ND Painting

P–PM LANGUAGE & LITERATURE
- PA Classical philology & lit.
- PC Romance languages
- PS–PF Germanic languages
- PE English philology
- PG Slavic languages (& lit.)
- PK Indo–Iranian languages
- PM 1–7356 Indians (American)

PN–PZ LANGUAGE & LITERATURE
- PN 1991–2 Radio &TV
- PN 1992–9 Moving pictures (Film)
- PN 2000–3299 Theater
- PN 4700–5650 Journalism
- PQ 1–3999 French literature
- PQ 4001–4999 Italian literature
- PQ 6001–8929 Spanish literature
- PQ 9000–9999 Portuguese literature
- PR English literature
- PR 2750–3112 Shakespeare
- PS American literature
- PT Germanic literature
- PZ (Juvenile) fiction

Q SCIENCE
- QA Mathematics
- QB Astronomy
- QC Physics
- QD Chemistry
- GE Geology
- QH–QR Biology
- QK Botany
- QL Zoology
- QP Physiology
- QR Bacteriology

R MEDICINE
- RA Hygiene, Public, Medicine, State
- RA 960–966 Hospitals
- RB Pathology
- RC Medicine–Practice
- RC 321–630 Psychiatry & Psychotherapy
- RC 423–7 Speech, Disorders of
- RJ Children–diseases
- RM Therapeutics. Pharmacology
- RM 214–259 Diet/therapeutics
- RT Nurses & Nursing

S AGRICULTURE
- SB Plants, Cultivated
- SD Forests & forestry
- SF Domestic animals
- SH Fisheries
- SK Hunting, camping

T TECHNOLOGY
- T–TX Industrial Arts
- TA–TK (Engineering)
- TL 1–445 Automobiles
- TL 500–830 Aeronautics
- TN Mines & mineral resources
- TP Chemistry, Technical
- TR Photography
- TS Manufactures
- TT Handicraft. Art metal-work
- TX Home economics

U MILITARY SCIENCE

V NAVAL SCIENCE

Z BIBLIOGRAPHY & LIBRARY SCIENCE
- Z 116–550 Book industries
- Z 124–242 Printing—history
- Z 551–656 Copyright
- Z 665–718 Library Science
- Z 1201–1929 American bibliography
- Z 2001–2029 Eng. Lit. bibliography
- Z 6941–6063 Periodicals bibliography
- Z 8811–8813 Shakespeare bibliography

BEGIN THE RESEARCH BY EXAMINING BOOKS

Locate the CARD CATALOGUE in the college or public library. A large majority of colleges employ The Library of Congress Classification System listed on pages 21–23 in this Guide.

Most libraries have a divided CARD CATALOGUE, one side being the AUTHOR/TITLE CATALOGUE and the other the SUBJECT CATALOGUE. If you have a literary research paper assignment, and you have decided to work on one aspect of the novels of D. H. Lawrence, you will find in the SUBJECT CATALOGUE a complete list of the books devoted to the life and work of D. H. Lawrence. (See examples of SUBJECT CARDS in this Guide). If you wish to look up the titles of all the novels by D. H. Lawrence, you will find those titles in the AUTHOR/TITLE CATALOGUE. (See examples of AUTHOR/TITLE CARDS also in this Guide).

Author card

BF
637
C45
W3

Watzlawick, Paul.

Pragmatics of human communication; a study of interactional patterns, pathologies, and paradoxes [by] Paul Watzlawick, Janet Helmick Beavin [and] Don D. Jackson. [1st ed.] New York, Norton [1967]

296 p. 22 cm.

"References": p. 272–283.

1. Communication. I. Beavin, Janet Helmick, joint author. II. Jackson, Donald De Avila, 1920– joint author. III. Title.

BF637.C45W3 152.3′84 67—11095

Library of Congress [68f5]

Title card

BF 637 C45 W3

Pragmatics of human communication

Watzlawick, Paul.

Pragmatics of human communication; a study of interactional patterns, pathologies, and paradoxes [by] Paul Watzlawick, Janet Helmick Beavin [and] Don D. Jackson. [1st ed.] New York, Norton [1967]

296 p. 22 cm.

"References": p. 272–283.

1. Communication. I. Beavin, Janet Helmick, joint author. II. Jackson, Donald De Avila, 1920– joint author. III. Title.

BF637.C45W3 152.3′84 67—11095

Library of Congress [68f5]

Subject card

BF 637 C45 W3

COMMUNICATION

Watzlawick, Paul.

Pragmatics of human communication; a study of interactional patterns, pathologies, and paradoxes [by] Paul Watzlawick, Janet Helmick Beavin [and] Don D. Jackson. [1st ed.] New York, Norton [1967]

296 p. 22 cm.

"References": p. 272–283.

1. Communication. I. Beavin, Janet Helmick, joint author. II. Jackson, Donald De Avila, 1920– joint author. III. Title.

BF637.C45W3 152.3′84 67—11095

Library of Congress [68f5]

Author card

PS Miller, Perry, 1905- ed.
682 American thought Civil War to World War 1.
M5 New York, Rinehart [1954]

lxii, 345 p. 19 cm. (Rinehart editions,70)

c.1

PS American thought: Civil War to World War 1
682 **Miller, Perry,** 1905- *ed.* *Title card*
M5 American thought: Civil War to World War I. New York, Rinehart [1954]

lxii, 345 p. 19 cm. (Rinehart editions, 70)

Bibliography: p. lii- lix.

1. American essays. 2. U. S.—Civilization—Addresses, essays, lectures. I. Title.

PS682.M5 814.4082 54—7243 ‡

Library of Congres [a64y½]

PS
682
M5

U. S. - CIVILIZATION - ADDRESSES, ESSAYS, LECTURES

Subject card

Miller, Perry, 1905–63 *ed.*

American thought: Civil War to World War I. New York, Rinehart [1954]

lxii, 345 p. 19 cm. (Rinehart editions, 70)

Bibliography: p. liii- lix.

✓1. American essays. ✓2. U. S.—Civilization—Addresses, essays, lectures. ✓I. Title.

PS682.M5 814.4082 54—7243 ‡

Library of Congress [a64y½]

AMERICAN ESSAYS

Subject card

PS
682
M5

Miller, Perry, 1905– *ed.*

American thought: Civil War to World War I. New York, Rinehart [1954]

lxii, 345 p. 19 cm. (Rinehart editions, 70)

Bibliography: p. liii- lix.

1. American essays. 2. U. S.—Civilization—Addresses, essays, lectures. I. Title.

PS682.M5 814.4082 54—7243 ‡

Library of Congress [a64y½]

ANOTHER APPROACH TO THE RESEARCH TOPIC: BEGIN WITH INDEXES TO PERIODICALS, MAGAZINES, REVIEWS, PERIODICALS, MAGAZINES, REVIEWS, SCHOLARLY JOURNALS

If you are working on a current topic such as abortion, for instance, the best index to begin with is the READERS' GUIDE TO PERIODICAL LITERATURE published by the H. W. Wilson Company of New York. The Readers' Guide is an index for the GENERAL READER and RESEARCHER and indexes 177 popular magazines such as Time, U.S. News and World Report, Field & Stream, Fortune, Psychology Today, Sports Illustrated, and many more. LOOK UNDER BOTH THE SUBJECT AND UNDER THE NAMES OF AUTHORS AND OTHER PEOPLE WHO MIGHT BE INVOLVED IN YOUR PAPER.

Sample Entries from the Readers' Guide

subject

CHILD abuse
author

Violent American way of life. W. Schuman. il → illustrations

Parents 55:60–70 S '80 ← volume, pages, date: Sept. 1980

title of article — name of periodical

subject

BLACKS ← title of article

Tampering with genes: a new threat to blacks?

R. Harris. il Ebony 35:31–4 S '80 ← pages, date, Sept. 1980 ← volume

author — illustrations — name of periodical

subject

HOPPER, Edward

Art. J. Ashberry por N Y 13:38–39 S 22 '80 ← volume, pages, date

author — portrait — name of periodical

Sample Entries from the Readers' Guide

author

Jerome, Fred

Science news: breaking the silence barrier. il → illustrated

Technol Rev 87: 8–9+ Jl '84

volume → pages, date: July 1984

title — name of periodical

If you are writing a scholarly research paper in psychology, anthropology, sociology, business, economics, education, geography, or political science, you may wish to begin your search for periodicals in the SOCIAL SCIENCE INDEX, which includes sources which are more scholarly than those indexed in the Readers' Guide. Look under SUBJECTS AND AUTHORS.

Sample Entries from the Social Science Index

subject

Gangs — title — author — (bibliography) included

Residence and territoriality in Chicano gangs. J. Moore and others. bibl Soc Prob 31:182–94 D '83

date: December 1983 — pages — volume — title of periodical

Galbraith, John Kenneth

Our debt to Ronald. New Statesm 106:14–16 N 24 '83

On the other hand, if you are preparing a scholarly research paper on any of the humanities such as literature, music, art, philosophy, architecture, dance, and religion, the HUMANITIES INDEX is a splendid source. Look under SUBJECTS AND AUTHORS.

Sample Entries from the Humanities Index

Garcia Lorca, Federico 1898–1936

about

Lorca in metamorphosis: his posthumous plays. F. H. Londre. Theatre J 35:102–108 Mr '83

Garland, Patricia A.

Three holocaust writers: speaking the unspeakable. *Critique* 24:45–56 Fall '83

Clarke, Christopher M.

Rejuvenation, reorganization and the dilemmas of modernization in post-Deng China. J Int Aff 39:119–32 Wint '86

Another index which may be of value in your research on literature, humanities, and social sciences is the ESSAY AND GENERAL LITERATURE INDEX published monthly and like the other indexes described here it is available in the REFERENCE SECTION of most college and public libraries. Important, well-known essays originally published in many scholarly journals and periodicals are usually reprinted, at a later date, in hard-cover anthologies or collections of essays. These essays which appear in books usually held by most libraries cannot be found in the CARD CATALOGUE, only in THE ESSAY AND GENERAL LITERATURE INDEX. An important research source, this index is often neglected as some students do not know of its existence. LOOK UNDER SUBJECTS AND AUTHORS.

Sample Entries from the Essay and General Literature Index

Psychology

Hediger, H. Do you speak Yerkish? The newest colloquial language with chimpanzees. In Speaking of apes, ed. by T. A. Sebeok and J. Umiker-Sebeok p331–51

Hill, J. H. Apes and language. In Speaking of apes by T. A. Sebeok and J. Umiker-Sebeok p441–47

Kellog, W. N. Communication and language in the home-raised chimpanzee. In Speaking of apes, ed. by T. A. Sebeok and J. Umiker-Sebeok

After finding the references above under Psychology in the main Index, turn to the back of the Index to LIST OF BOOKS INDEXED. In that list under the title of Speaking of Apes, the following data appears:

Call number:

QL737 P96 S63 (Library of Congress System. Zoology is indexed under QL).	Speaking of apes: a critical anthology of two-way communication with man. Ed. by Thomas A. Sebeok and Jean Umiker-Sebeok. Plenum Press 1980 480p (Topics in contemporary semiotics) ISBN 0–306–40279–3 LC 79–17714

Furthermore, for students interested in psychology, the PSYCHOLOGICAL ABSTRACTS are a most valuable source for a scholarly paper in any aspect of psychology.

For instance, a student's assignment is to research one apsect of "psychokinesis." If this subject gives the researcher a problem, the student should consult the LIBRARY OF CONGRESS SUBJECT INDEX to be found usually at the main Reference Desk of the library. The Library of Congress Subject Index does list "psychokinesis" and suggests that the researcher also see the topics of parapsychology, levitation, and spiritualism.

First, the student should look in the PSYCHOLOGICAL ABSTRACTS INDEX such as the INDEX for January–June 1982. In that Index one finds:

Psychokinses
Cox Plaster Box & Cox Cubeless Coffeebox, measures of psychokinesis effects, 16

In the PSYCHOLOGICAL ABSTRACTS themselves, one finds the volume for January 1982, Volume 67, Number 1, since the original reference to the Cox Plaster Box & Cox Cubeless Coffeebox appears in the INDEX of January–June 1982, VOLUME 67. The researcher then looks under number 16, the number following the title of the article on Cox Plaster Box & Cox Cubeless Coffeebox. On page 2 of VOLUME 67, January 1982 appears:

16. Richards, John T. (Columbia Coll, MO) Paranormal sine curve tracing the Cox Cubeless Coffeebox. Parapsychology Review 1980 (Jul–Aug), Vol 11 (4), 23–24. Introduces 2 new devices (the Cox Plaster Box and Cox Cubeless Coffeebox) that measure psychokinesis (PK) effects and relates an experiment involving the latter. Results indicate that no target cube is necessary to produce PK tracing effects and that some "conscious" control of PK is possible.

Newspaper Indexes

Newspapers are usual tools in researching both current, popular topics as well as scholarly subjects. The following distinguished newspapers are considered both popular and scholarly sources:

NEW YORK TIMES
WALL STREET JOURNAL
LOS ANGELES TIMES
WASHINGTON POST
CHRISTIAN SCIENCE MONITOR

THE NEW YORK TIMES INDEX is published separately and is owned by most libraries. College libraries generally own a complete set of all copies of the New York Times from the beginning of publication (1851) until today, a complete run that has been reproduced on microfilm. Here is an example from the New York Times from the Index of May 16–31, 1984:

subject → KING, Martin Luther Jr. (1929–68)
Photo of marchers trooping up Fifth Avenue in 17th memorial march for slain civil rights leader Martin Luther King Jr. My 21, II, 2:5 → page 2, column 5
→ section II
month: May 21 (1984)

Some large college and public libraries own the NEWSPAPER INDEX which indexes the Wall Street Journal, New York Times, Los Angeles Times, Washington Post, and the Christian Science Monitor, all in one index, cumulated monthly.

You should also consult the Reference Librarian about pamphlet indexes, microfilms, and the computer databases.

1. GENERAL REFERENCE WORKS

A. General

Bartlett, John. FAMILIAR QUOTATIONS. 15th edition. Boston: Little, Brown, 1980. (125th Anniversary Edition)

FACTS ON FILE. New York: Facts on File, Inc., 1940–date
(Published Weekly with annual cumulation)

STATESMAN'S YEARBOOK: STATISTICAL & HISTORICAL ANNUAL OF THE STATES OF THE WORLD. New York: St. Martin's Press, 1985–1986.
(Published annually since 1864)

STATISTICAL ABSTRACT OF THE UNITED STATES: NATIONAL DATA BOOK AND GUIDE TO SOURCES. Washington, D. C.: United States Department of Commerce, Census Bureau, 1986.
(Published annually since 1880)

WORLD ALMANAC AND BOOK OF FACTS. New York: Newspaper Enterprise Association, 1868–1987. (Annual)

B. Atlases

ATLAS OF AMERICAN HISTORY. 2nd revised edition. New York: Charles Scribner's Sons, 1984.

COLUMBIA-LIPPINCOTT GAZETTEER OF THE WORLD. New York: Columbia University and the American Geographical Society, 1952.

RAND MC NALLY COMMERCIAL ATLAS AND MARKETING GUIDE. Chicago: Rand Mc Nally and Company, Inc., 1986. (Published annually)

TIMES ATLAS OF THE WORLD. New York: Times Books, 1985.

C. Biography

BIOGRAPHY INDEX: A Cumulative Index To Biographical Material in Books and Magazines. New York: H. W. Wilson, 1946–date.

CHAMBERS' BIOGRAPHICAL DICTIONARY. Edited by J. O. Thorne and T. C. Collocott. New York: Cambridge University Press, 1984.

CURRENT BIOGRAPHY. New York: H. W. Wilson, 1940–date.
(Monthly with annual cumulation)

DICTIONARY OF AMERICAN BIOGRAPHY (DAB). New York: Charles Schribner's Sons, 1958–1981. (26 volumes)

DICTIONARY OF NATIONAL BIOGRAPHY (DNB). London: Oxford University Press, 1882–1981. (27 volumes)

WHO'S WHO IN AMERICA. Chicago: Marquis Who's Who, 1899–1986. (Annual)

WHO'S WHO. New York: St. Martin's Press, 1848–date. (Annual)

D. Dictionaries

DICTIONARIES OF AMERICAN ENGLISH; based upon Webster's New World Dictionary of the American Language. New York: Simon and Schuster, 1981.

Fowler, Henry Watson. A DICTIONARY OF MODERN ENGLISH USAGE. 2d ed. New York: Oxford University Press, 1983.

OXFORD ENGLISH DICTIONARY (OED) Oxford: at the Clarendon Press, 1933–1986. (17 volumes)

Partridge, Eric. A DICTIONARY OF SLANG AND UNCONVENTIONAL ENGLISH. London: Routledge & Kegan Paul, 1984.

ROGET'S INTERNATIONAL THESAURUS. 4th ed. New York: Harper & Row, 1984.

WEBSTER'S THIRD NEW INTERNATIONAL DICTIONARY. Springfield, Massachusetts: G. & C. Merriam Company, 1966.

E. Encyclopedias

ENCYCLOPEDIA BRITANNICA. Chicago: Encyclopedia Britannica, Inc, 1768–1986.

ENCYCLOPEDIA AMERICANA. Chicago: Encyclopedia Americana, 1829–1986.

COLLIER'S ENCYCLOPEDIA. New York: Macmillan Educational Corporation, 1986.

WORLD BOOK ENCYCLOPEDIA. Chicago: World Book, Inc., 1917–1986.

The above encyclopedias update at least 10% each year. In addition, each company publishes a yearbook to supplement the encyclopedia.

F. INDEXES

BIBLIOGRAPHIC INDEX: A CUMULATIVE BIBLIOGRAPHY OF BIBLIOGRAPHIES. New York: H. W. Wilson, 1938–date.

BOOK REVIEW DIGEST. New York: H. W. Wilson, 1905–date.

ESSAY AND GENERAL LITERATURE INDEX. New York: H. W. Wilson, 1900–date.

MLA INTERNATIONAL BIBLIOGRAPHY. New York: Modern Language Association, 1963–date.

NEW YORK TIMES INDEX. New York: The New York Times Company, 1851–date.

PUBLIC AFFAIRS INFORMATION SERVICE. New York: P.A.I.S., 1915–date.

READERS' GUIDE TO PERIODICAL LITERATURE. New York: H. W. Wilson, 1900–date.

United States. MONTHLY CATALOG OF U. S. GOVERNMENT PUBLICATIONS. Washington, D. C.: United States Government Printing Office, 1895–date.

2. NATURAL SCIENCES

A. General

DICTIONARY OF SCIENTIFIC BIOGRAPHY. New York: Charles Schribner's Sons, 1976 (13 volumes)

GENERAL SCIENCE INDEX. New York: H. W. Wilson, 1979–date.

MC GRAW-HILL ENCYCLOPEDIA OF SCIENCE & TECHNOLOGY, 6th ed. New York: Mc Graw-Hill, 1986.

VAN NOSTRAND'S SCIENTIFIC ENCYCLOPEDIA, 6th ed. New York: Van Nostrand & Company, 1983.

B. Agriculture

AGRICULTURAL STATISTICS. Washington, D. C.: United States Department of Agriculture. (Annual)

BIBLIOGRAPHY OF AGRICULTURE. Phoenix, Arizona: Oryx Press, 1942–date.

YEARBOOK OF AGRICULTURE. Washington, D. C., United States Department of Agriculture. (Annual)

C. Applied Science

APPLIED SCIENCE AND TECHNOLOGY INDEX. New York: H. W. Wilson, 1958–date.

ENGINEERING INDEX MONTHLY AND AUTHOR INDEX. New York: Engineering Information, Inc., 1884–date.

D. Biology

BIOLOGICAL AND AGRICULTURAL INDEX. New York: H. W. Wilson, 1916–date.

ENCYCLOPEDIA OF THE BIOLOGICAL SCIENCES. Edited by Peter Gray. New York: Van Nostrand and Company, Inc., 1981.

INDEX MEDICUS. Washington, D. C.: National Library of Medicine, 1927–date.

MERCK INDEX: an encyclopedia of chemicals, drugs and biologicals. 10th ed. Rahway, N.J.: Merck & Company, 1983.

PHYSICIAN'S DESK REFERENCE. Oradell, N.J.: Medical Economics, Inc. (Annual)

PROGRESS IN BIOPHYSICS AND MOLECULAR BIOLOGY. New York: Pergamon, 1950–date.

E. Chemistry

CHEMICAL ABSTRACTS. Columbus, Ohio: American Chemical Society, 1907–date.

ENCYCLOPEDIA OF CHEMICAL TECHNOLOGY. 3d ed. New York: Wiley, 1980.

HANDBOOK OF CHEMISTRY AND PHYSICS. 65th ed. Boca Raton, Florida: CRC Press, 1984.

LANGE'S HANDBOOK OF CHEMISTRY. 13th ed. New York: McGraw-Hill, 1985.

VAN NOSTRAND'S CHEMICAL ANNUAL. New York: Van Nostrand & Company, Inc., 1907–date.

F. GEOLOGY

GEOLOGICAL SOCIETY OF AMERICA. ABSTRACTS. Boulder, Colorado: The Society, 1919–date.

MINERALS YEARBOOK. Washington, D. C.: United States Department of the Interior, 1933–date. (Annual)

G. Physics and Mathematics

Chemical Rubber Company. STANDARD MATHEMATICAL TABLES. Cleveland, Ohio: The Company, 1984.

ENCYCLOPAEDIC DICTIONARY OF PHYSICS. New York: Pergamon Press, 1966–1984.
(Base volumes with supplements)

Glenn, James. DICTIONARY OF MATHEMATICS. New York: Barnes & Noble, 1984.

REVIEWS OF MODERN PHYSICS. New York: American Institute of Physics, 1929–date.

3. SOCIAL SCIENCES

A. General

ENCYCLOPEDIA OF THE SOCIAL SCIENCES. New York: Macmillan, 1930.

INTERNATIONAL ENCYCLOPEDIA OF THE SOCIAL SCIENCES. New York: Macmillan and Free Press, 1968.

Koschnik, Wolfgang. DICTIONARY OF THE SOCIAL SCIENCES. New York: K. G. Saur, 1984.

SOCIAL SCIENCES INDEX. New York: H. W. Wilson, 1974–date.

B. Business

BUSINESS PERIODICALS INDEX. New York: H. W. Wilson, 1958–date.

MILLION DOLLAR DIRECTORY. Parsippany, N.J.: Dun & Bradstreet Corporation, (Annual)

MOODY'S INVESTORS SERVICES. New York: Moody's Investors Service. (Looseleaf twice weekly, cumulated annually)

STANDARD & POOR'S CORPORATION RECORDS. New York: Standard & Poor, 1928–date.

STANDARD & POOR'S REGISTER OF CORPORATIONS, DIRECTORS & EXECUTIVES, UNITED STATES AND CANADA. New York: Standard & Poor, 1928–date.

WALL STREET JOURNAL INDEX. New York: Dow Jones, 1958–date.

C. Economics

Moffat, Donald W. ECONOMICS DICTIONARY. 2nd ed. New York: Elsevier, 1984.

REVIEW OF ECONOMICS AND STATISTICS. The Netherlands: North Holland Publishing Company, 1919–date.

D. Education

CURRENT INDEX TO JOURNALS IN EDUCATION (CIJE). Phoenix, Arizona: Oryx Press, 1969–date.

INTERNATIONAL ENCYCLOPEDIA OF EDUCATION, RESEARCH AND STUDIES. New York: Pergamon Press, 1985.

RESOURCES IN EDUCATION. Bethesda, Maryland: United States Department of Education, 1975–date.

E. Geography

WEBSTER'S NEW GEOGRAPHICAL DICTIONARY. Springfield, Massachusetts: Merriam-Webster, 1984.

WORLDMARK ENCYCLOPEDIA OF THE NATIONS. New York: Wiley, 1984.

F. History

The CAMBRIDGE HISTORIES (Ancient, Medieval, Modern). Cambridge: Cambridge University Press, 1911–1979.

DICTIONARY OF AMERICAN HISTORY. New York: Charles Schribner's Sons, 1976.

HARVARD GUIDE TO AMERICAN HISTORY. Cambridge, Massachusetts: Belknap Press of Harvard University, 1976.

HISTORICAL ABSTRACTS. Santa Barbara, California: CLIO Press, 1955–date.

G. Political Science

CONGRESSIONAL QUARTERLY ALMANAC. Washington, D. C.: CQ, Inc. (Annual)
(Looseleaf weekly with annual cumulation)

ENCYCLOPEDIA OF AMERICAN POLITICAL HISTORY. Edited by Jack P. Greene. New York: Charles Scribner's Sons, 1984.

FOREIGN RELATIONS OF THE UNITED STATES. Washington, D. C.: United States Government Printing Office, 1925–date.

Plano, Jack. AMERICAN POLITICAL DICTIONARY. 7th ed. New York: Holt, Rinehart, Winston, 1985.

POLITICAL HANDBOOK OF THE WORLD. Binghamton, New York: CSA (SUNY–Binghamton) 1927–date.

H. Psychology

Chaplin, J. P. DICTIONARY OF PSYCHOLOGY. 3rd ed. New York: Dell, 1985.

Eysenck, H. J. ENCYCLOPEDIA OF PSYCHOLOGY. 2nd ed. New York: Continuim, 1979.

PSYCHOLOGICAL ABSTRACTS. Washington, D.C.: American Psychological Association, 1927–date.

I. Sociology

Abercrombie, Nicholas. PENGUIN DICTIONARY OF SOCIOLOGY. New York: Penguin, 1984.

SOCIAL SCIENCES CITATION INDEX. Philadelphia: Institute for Scientific Information, 1969–date.

SOCIAL SCIENCES INDEX. New York: H. W. Wilson, 1974–date.

SOCIOLOGICAL ABSTRACTS. San Diego, California: International Sociological Association, 1953–date.

4. HUMANITIES

A. Art and Architecture

ART INDEX. New York: H. W. Wilson, 1929–date.

ENCYCLOPEDIA OF WORLD ART. Palatine, Illinois: Publishers Guild, 1959.

Haggar, Reginald G. DICTIONARY OF ART TERMS. New York: Sterling, 1985.

MACMILLAN ENCYLCLOPEDIA OF ARCHITECTS. New York: Free Press, 1982. (4 volumes)

B. Literature

ABSTRACTS OF ENGLISH STUDIES. Calgary, Canada: University of Calgary, 1958–date.

CONTEMPORARY AUTHORS. Chicago: Gale, 1964–date. (110 volumes)

HUMANITIES INDEX. New York: H. W. Wilson, 1974–date.

MC GRAW-HILL ENCYCLOPEDIA OF WORLD DRAMA. New York: McGraw-Hill, 1984. (5 volumes)

OXFORD COMPANION TO AMERICAN LITERATURE. 5th ed. New York: Oxford, 1983.

OXFORD COMPANION TO ENGLISH LITERATURE. 5th ed. New York: Oxford, 1983.

C. Music and Dance

ENCYCLOPEDIA OF JAZZ. New York: Horizon, 1960–1976. (3 volumes)

GROVE'S DICTIONARY OF MUSIC AND MUSICIANS. New York: Grove, 1986.

HARVARD DICTIONARY OF MUSIC. Cambridge, Massachusetts: Belknap Press of Harvard, 1986.

INTERNATIONAL CYCLOPEDIA OF MUSIC AND MUSICIANS. 11th ed. New York: Dodd, Mead, 1983.

D. Philosophy and Religion

Eliade, Mircea. ENCYCLOPEDIA OF RELIGION. New York: Macmillan, 1986. (16 volumes)

ENCYCLOPEDIA OF PHILOSOPHY. New York: Macmillan, 1967. (8 volumes)

Hastings, James. ENCYCLOPEDIA OF RELIGION AND ETHICS. New York: Charles Scribner's Sons, 1962.

Keter Publishing House (Jerusalem). ENCYCLOPEDIA JUDAICA. New York: Macmillan, 1972.

NEW CATHOLIC ENCYCLOPEDIA. New York, McGraw-Hill, 1967.

PHILOSOPHER'S INDEX. An international index to philosophical periodicals and the philosophy research archives. Bowling Green, Ohio: Bowling Green University, Philosophy Department, 1967–date.

FOURTH SESSION

Making Note Cards

PART TWO

If you are an inexperienced researcher, you may have been told or you may believe that taking notes on cards is "busy work," and therefore, not important. You are wrong in this regard. NOTE CARDS ARE ESSENTIAL TO THE SUCCESS OF THE RESEARCH PAPER, FOR CORRECT NOTE CARDS ARE RELATED TO THE OUTLINE OF THE RESEARCH PAPER AND THE ORGANIZATION OF THE RESEARCH PAPER. You should, therefore, make a note card for every source you wish to include in the paper. YOU SHOULD USE A FIVE INCH BY SEVEN INCH (5″ × 7″) CARD AVAILABLE IN THE COLLEGE BOOKSTORE. When you have completed a stack of note cards, you can easily read through them and ascertain the kind of research paper the note cards tend to suggest. (See Fifth Session, Part Two). For example, you are writing on the misogyny of August Strindberg (the hatred of women). When you study your note cards, it becomes obvious that the data you have gathered on Strindberg's misogyny, from primary and secondary sources, can be traced from his early adolescence through his middle and later years. Your note cards also indicate that the theme of misogyny is prevalent in his early plays and stories and in the later work as well. The note cards lead you to see that ANALYSIS BY CHRONOLOGY, or organization through the process of time, is the type of organization suited to the topic. The next step is to make the outline, and the note cards seem to fall into FIVE MAJOR SECTIONS (I, II, III, IV, and V) to correspond to the CHRONOLOGICAL PERIODS IN STRINDBERG'S LIFE. With the outline completed, it is a simple task to use a MAGIC MARKER PEN to divide the note cards into the five chronological sections (I, II, III, IV, and V). After the markings are done, it is simple to sort these note cards into five stacks, according to I, II, III, IV, and V. Then it is a relatively easy matter to write the paper following the materials you have gathered on the cards. NOTE CARDS SHOULD BE WRITTEN IN INK, ON ONE SIDE OF THE CARD ONLY.

If you have only a vague idea about the outline of the research paper and you have prepared no note cards, the task of writing your paper will be complicated, if not impossible. For an experiment in confusion and hopelessness, try to organize and write a research paper from smudgy pencil scrawls written on all sizes and kinds of paper, on both sides; from xerox copies of articles and books, xerox copies that are illegible; from many books which lie strewn about your room, books into which you have thrust flimsy paper markers to locate certain important passages, from notes to yourself written on the college cafeteria paper napkins; and from various other kinds of data jotted on a variety of sheets and papers, some dirty, some stained, all illegible. It is obvious that this experiment is doomed to failure. INDEED, NOTE CARDS IN INK AND ON ONE SIDE OF THE CARD ONLY, ARRANGED PROPERLY (SEE EXAMPLES OF NOTE-CARDS IN THE FOLLOWING PAGES) ARE THE BEST SOLUTION TO WRITING AND ORGANIZING A GOOD RESEARCH PAPER.

Furthermore, you should make a smaller note card for every source you wish to include. YOU SHOULD USE A THREE BY FIVE INCH (3″ × 5″) CARD AVAILABLE IN THE COLLEGE BOOKSTORE. This card can be used as a bibliography card which will be helpful in preparing the "Works Cited" Section. After you have made a bibliography card for each source, it is a simple matter to arrange these cards ALPHABETICALLY, a process to facilitate the "Works Cited."

Represents a 5X7 card

WRITE ON ONE SIDE ONLY

PRIMARY SOURCE CARD

D. H. Lawrence Sons and Lovers (22-23)
Short quotations and paraphrase.
The Morels are having a fierce battle when Mr. Morel arrives home from work, drunk. He contends he spends very little on drink (SL 22).
"You don't get as drunk as a lord on nothing," she replied. "And," she cried, "flashing with sudden fury, "if you've been sponging on your beloved Jerry, why not let him look after his own children, for they need it (SL 22).
"It's a lie, it's a lie. Shut your face, woman." They were now at battle pitch. (SL 22).

Represents a 5X7 card

WRITE ON ONE SIDE ONLY

SECONDARY SOURCE CARD

"On Sons and Lovers by Dorothy Van Ghent. In D. H. Lawrence: A Collection of Critical Essays. Englewood Cliffs, N.J.: Prentice 1963. Long quotation: ". . . but that it (S and L) (15-28) has a structure rigorously controlled by an idea: an idea of an organic disturbance in the relationships of men and women—a disturbance of sexual polarities that is seen in the disaffection of mother and father, then in the mother's attempt to substitute her sons for her husband, finally in the sons' unsuccessful struggle to establish natural manhood" (17-18).

Represents a 5X7 card

WRITE ON ONE SIDE ONLY

SECONDARY SOURCE CARD

Paraphrase

"On Sons and Lovers" by Dorothy Van Ghent (17).
This offense against biological rhythms comes about in Mrs. Morel, Paul, and Miriam because each fails to respect the personal individuality of the other [his her freedom, etc]. Each tries to possess the other: Mrs. Morel wants to possess Mr. Morel and her sons, particularly William and Paul; and Miriam tries to possess Paul. Also doesn't Clara try to possess and control Paul?

Represents a 5X7 card

WRITE ON ONE SIDE ONLY

SECONDARY SOURCE CARD

Short quotation and paraphrase (17).
"Lawrence saw this offense [possession] as a disease [emphasis mine] of modern life in all its manifestations, from sexual... to social and political relationships that have changed people to... anonymous automations" (17).
(paraphrase): This theme of possession can be seen in the narrative of the novel and in the imagery (17).
My personal comment. Make connections to scene with Mrs. Morel (SL) and her lilies. re: possession.

Write a bibliography card for the "Works Cited" page (MLA) or for "References" (APA), a card for every source you use.

Lawrence, D. H. Sons and Lovers. 1913.
New York: Penguin, 1981.

MLA
BOOK

These cards represent 3 X 5 note cards

Schorer, Mark. <u>D. H. Lawrence</u>. New
York: Dell, 1968

MLA
<u>BOOK</u>

Hough, Graham. <u>The
Dark Sun: A Study
of D. H. Lawrence.</u>
London: Duckworth,
1956.

MLA
<u>BOOK</u>

Van Ghent, Dorothy. "On Sons and Lovers." In D. H. Lawrence: A Collection of Critical Essays. Ed. Mark Spilka. Englewood Cliffs, N. J.: Prentice, 1963.

MLA
ARTICLE IN BOOK

Aldridge, John W. "D. H. Lawrence's Sensibility." In Critiques and Essays in Modern Fiction. Ed. Aldridge. New York: Ronald, 1952. 328-332.

MLA
ARTICLE

Freehill, M. (1973)
Disturbed and troubled
children. New York:
Saunders.

APA
BOOK

Segal, J. and Segal, Z.
(1986, February) When your
kids won't go to school
Parents, p. 152.

APA
ARTICLE

FIFTH SESSION

The Introduction and Thesis as Well as the Conclusion

PART ONE

The introduction to the research paper is essential. The writer of the paper does not necessarily begin the paper with the thesis sentence but with an introduction which should include the thesis statement which may be implicit or explicit. The thesis sentence or idea should be included within the first paragraph of the paper, if possible, and if not in the first, then in the second. The thesis idea should be included on the first page of the paper. THE TITLE OF THE RESEARCH PAPER SHOULD INCLUDE AN ABBREVIATED STATEMENT OF THE THESIS ITSELF. The thesis of a paper is a position or proposition the writer advances, a theory or idea he or she wishes to explore and/or prove; in other words, the thesis statement announces the content of the research paper, particularly when the thesis idea is an explicit one rather than implicit. THE THESIS TOPIC OR IDEA IS A NARROW ASPECT OF A LARGER SUBJECT. "The Life and Work of Ernest Hemingway" is <u>not</u> an appropriate thesis or topic to be covered in six to ten pages, the average length of an undergraduate college research essay. A more narrow aspect of that broad Hemingway idea might be: "Ernest Hemingway: The Transcendental Hero : 'Big Two-Hearted River, Parts I and II', and 'Indian Camp.' "

Examples of the Explicit Thesis

This report will explore how EMG (electromyographic) biofeedback, coupled with other techniques of relaxation, aids in the cure or relief of everyday emotional problems such as tension headaches, insomnia, subvocalization, psychosomatic problems, such as hypertension and gastrointestinal disorders, and finally, physical problems such as neuromuscular injuries and migraine headaches.

Suggested Title for the Paper Dealing with the Thesis above

EMG Biofeedback: The Drugless Cure.

Another Explicit Thesis

The purpose of this paper is to explore the ways in which John Gardner (1933–1982) deals with the question of human values in his adaptation of the "Beowulf" myth in his existential novel <u>Grendel</u> (1971).

Suggested Title for the Paper Dealing with the Thesis above

John Gardner's Adaptation of the 'Beowulf' Myth in : <u>Grendel</u>

Another Explicit Thesis

The aim here is to explore the causes and effects of <u>rumor</u> in regard to psychological and sociological behavior.

Suggested Title for This Paper

Socio-Psychological Dynamics of Rumor: Causes and Effects.

Another Explicit Thesis

The aim of this paper is to demonstrate how Euripides, Lope de Vega, Racine, and Jeffers examined and dealt with the principal conflict between the mythological Hippolytus and Phaedra in several of their fictional works.

Suggested Title for This Paper

The Hippolytus Myth: Euripides, Lope de Vega, Racine, and Jeffers

Examples of the Implicit Thesis

Had it not been for D. H. Lawrence's untimely death in 1930, the integration in him of puritanism and romanticism might have been achieved, but evidence indicates that, despite his genius, he had been deeply damaged emotionally as a result of his childhood. His youthful, traumatic experiences produced numerous contradictions in both his private and professional lives. A tremendous duality of opposing forces in the personality of Lawrence can be concluded. By his own admission, he was "two men inside one skin."

Suggested Title Dealing with the Thesis above

D. H. Lawrence: "Two Men Inside One Skin"

Another Implicit Thesis

The determinants of psychology have traditionally been sought in early childhood. Psychological investigations of social and historical processes are generally based on the commonly accepted view that psychological development begins postnatally. Stanislov Grof, Lloyd deMause and R. D. Laing have each developed theories of pre and peri-natal psychology. Each theorist has hypothesized that the structure of the psyche is an expression of a particular period of womb experience.

Suggested Title for this Paper:

Grof, de Mause, and Laing: The Expression of Pre and Perinatal Phenomenology

SOME DEVICES THAT MAY BE USED IN THE INTRODUCTION

1. The student writer's own words.

   This approach is fairly simple and widely used. The student, in his or her own words, writes in general terms about the idea or problem that the paper will deal with. (See examples further on.) However, since the research paper is not a personal essay, or an intimate piece dealing only with the student writer's own ideas, YOU SHOULD NOT USE THE PERSONAL PRONOUNS I—or—WE, or their objective forms—Me—or—US. For example, do not write: I think that one of the most difficult problems facing parents and teachers today in the lower grades is the definition of what is a gifted child. The I think is the grammatical subject of that sentence although the writer is not intentionally putting himself or herself forward. The writer is stressing the difficult problem of defining the gifted child. The I think calls too much attention to the writer rather than the gifted child. The I think is also DEADWOOD WHICH

VIOLATES THE OBJECTIVE, IMPARTIAL TONE OF A RESEARCH PAPER. Rather, you should write: One of the most difficult problems facing parents and teachers today in the lower grades is the definition of what is a gifted child. SINCE THIS STATEMENT HAS NO INTERNAL DOCUMENTATION, IT IS ASSUMED THAT IT IS THE STUDENT WRITER OF THE PAPER WHO IS MAKING THIS STATEMENT ABOUT THE PROBLEM OF DEFINING THE GIFTED CHILD. Likewise, never write: It is my opinion that, it seems to me that, it appears to me that, let me make this point, or let us proceed to the next point. IN OTHER WORDS, DO NOT WRITE I, WE, ME, AND US, AND CERTAINLY ONE MUST AVOID THE USE OF THE TOO GENERAL TERM "YOU." RESEARCH PAPERS ARE USUALLY WRITTEN IN THE THIRD PERSON SO THAT IF ONE INTERJECTS THE PRONOUN "YOU," THAT USAGE BREAKS THE THIRD-PERSON POINT OF VIEW. It is obvious that in the middle of a paper dealing with the gifted child one would not write: You know that you have a problem with gifted children. You see right off that such children must be instructed differently than the average student. This usage of "YOU" must be avoided.

WHEN THE STUDENT WRITER WISHES TO EXPRESS SOME OF HIS OR HER IDEAS IN HIS OR HER OWN WORDS, the student may do so in the following way: "And here no one can fail to perceive that when all has been weighed on the most delicate of scales, Emma Bovary has been truly denied by the circumstances of time."

Another Example

"One interprets that the boy's physical arrest and enclosure are symbolic of his spiritual paralysis that has been demonstrated previously. Like the two preceding stories of Joyce, 'The Sisters' is an excellent example of Joyce's central theme of spiritual and physical paralysis." <u>Furthermore</u>, <u>since the student's own interpretation of the materials at hand (FIRST SESSION, pages 1, 5–6) will have no internal documentation</u>, <u>the reader will naturally assume that these words are by the student writer of the paper</u>. An example of the student's own words without the use of <u>one</u> or <u>this writer</u> . . . finds that: "From the understanding of how CAT (computerized axial tomography) scans are accomplished, this procedure provides medicine with 'eyes' to make possible the detection and treatment of diseases. The scanner is useful in examining the brain, always a difficult area of study. The heart can be more carefully examined because the CAT scanner presents an image of the chambers of the heart and the flow of blood through the coronary arteries. It is, therefore, one of the safest, most painless and quickest wonders of modern medicine."

2. Short quotations and paraphrase along with some of the student's own words.
3. Long quotation.
4. Poem.
5. A series of questions.
6. Other devices such an analogy, anecdote, non sequitur, startling statement, etc.

SOME OF THESE DEVICES MAY BE USEFUL IN WRITING THE CONCLUSION OF THE RESEARCH PAPER (SEE END OF THIS SESSION).

The Increase in Violence:
Its Relation to "Anomie"

student's own words

Acts of criminal violence seem to be approaching epidemic proportions in society today. The technological, industrial, and commercial advancement of modern society, has perpetuated, and expanded, rather than suppressed, the violence associated with criminal behavior. In reference to morality, most people are aware that crime (robbery, assault, murder, rape, and almost all other acts of criminal violence), has undergone a transformation from bad to worse. The breakdown of morality is directly related to the social state of discontinuity or aimlessness associated with human behavior known as "anomie." Crime does not seem more violent today because of a sudden new sense of social awareness, or an escalation in public morality. Modern social structure, with its emphasis on success, and equality for all, is the cause of the growth of senseless violence or "anomic" behavior in our society.

thesis

In addition to viewing the growth of violent and non-violent crime, and providing a functional analysis of crime in society, the aim of this paper is to define "anomie" in terms of a sociological perspective, to show how criminal violence and moral degeneration are directly . . . .

short quotations and paraphrase

Anorexia Nervosa and Bulimia:
Fitting Society's Image

Love. Happiness. Success. She can have them all and more--if she is thin. That is the message being passed along to millions of women both here and abroad, through radio, magazine, television, and in conversations by society at-large. But does the message hold true? Not always. For many, the desire for the ultimate, thin figure leads only to years of lonely torture: obsessive dieting, laxative addiction, uncontrollable binging, and self-induced vomiting. Anorexia nervosa, the "starving disease," and bulimia, the "gorge-purge" syndrome, are eating disorders whose victims, according to Current Health (18) are 90 to 95 percent female. The aim, therefore, of this paper is to analyze anorexia nervosa and bulimia, serious eating disorders which Western society induces by promoting the "ultra-thin ideal woman" image.

thesis

"Anorexia nervosa," states Dr. Hilde Bruch, eminent authority on eating disorders, "is a distinct illness with an outstanding feature: relentless pursuit of excessive thinness" (7). Paradoxically, while the term anorexia nervosa denotes loss of appetite due to a nervous condition, the anorexic victim is actually obsessed . . . .

Steinbeck's Ma Joad and Zola's La Maheude:
Archetypal Earth-Mothers in *Grapes of Wrath*
and *Germinal*

long quotation

> Like other archetypes, the Earth-Mother is recognized by means of specific symbols she assumes in projection. She may appear not only as a personification of nature or the creative source, but also as a superhuman being or goddess--although this frequently is a personification through anthropomorphosis (the Virgin Mary, for example). She may also appear as an abstraction, disguised in the form of an ultimate ambition or goal, especially when the goal takes the form of a longing for Heaven or a deathwish; in these cases, overlapping with two other archetypes may occur: the Search and Return to the Womb. She may appear in the form of a politician, a religious or social institution that offers the protection of a collective identity. . . . (Evans and Finestone 57)

The above description which appears in *Archetypes in Action* further substantiates what Carl Gustave Jung points out: "Archetypes come to life only when one patiently tries to discover why and in what fashion they are meaningful to a living individual" (88). Both John Steinbeck (1902-1968) and Emile Zola (1840-1902) find the Earth-Mother archetype significant and create that archetype in The Grapes of Wrath (1939) and Germinal (1885) in the leading women protagonists, Ma Joad and La Maheude.

The fact that Ma Joad is an Earth-Mother is substantiated by Evans and Finestone (58), and La Maheude's being the same archetype is explained by Elliot Mansfield Grant, a literary critic, in his book Zola's Germinal (58).

thesis

"The Great Earth-Mother who brings forth all life from herself . . ." declares Erich Newman, a literary scholar, "is symbolized as a fruit-bearing tree of life" (58). Newman goes on to say that sprouting leaves, forming twigs, growing branches, transforming blossoms bearing fruit and nourishing roots, the tree is contained in itself and dependent on itself. The tree protects itself and because of its beautiful treetop, birds choose to live and reproduce in the leaves and branches. Reproducing is a function of both the treetop and the trunk (49). Ma Joad's extended family (or tree) consists of Pa, Granma, Granpa, Tom, Uncle John, Al, Ruthie, Winfield, Rose of Sharon, Noah, and Rose of Sharon's husband, Connie. On the other hand, La Maheude's family . . . .

The Poetry of Emily Dickinson:
Her Depiction of Motion and
Fixity in Nature

Some things that fly there be--
Birds--Hours--the Bumblebee--
Of these no Elegy.

Some things that stay there be--
Grief--Hills--Eternity--

Nor this behooveth me.

There are that resting, rise.
Can I expound the skies?
How still the Riddle lies!
(<u>The Complete Poems</u> 89).

Among the many fascinations Emily Dickinson (1830-1886) has with the natural world around her are the concepts of motion, fixity, and metamorphosis. David Porter, a well-known literary critic, suggests that "movement and change represent for Emily Dickinson the process by which one passes from personal isolation to consummate union, from artistic endeavor to literary immortality" (75). It is, therefore, the purpose of this paper to demonstrate, with the use of several of her poems, how Emily Dickinson's intrinsic curiosity about "things that fly," "things that stay," and in addition, those "that resting, rise" suggests an involvement with the ideas of motion and fixity. . . . .

. . . .

Childhood Dyslexia

a series of questions

He is a highly intelligent individual, yet his ideas do not translate from brain to paper. He tries to read, but somehow the figures on the page do not match the sounds he hears. Everyone else can read in school, but why can't he? Once aware of this inability, he becomes angered and frustrated, for he mistakes it as stupidity. Why does this occur? How can dyslexic children be so brilliant or creative, yet not have the ability to read or write? The purpose of this paper is to answer these questions, and to provide the reader with a basic knowledge of the perceptual disorder, dyslexia.

thesis

According to Rudolph C. Wagner, a noted developmental psychologist, the term 'dyslexia' is referred to as ". . . a disturbed function of the symbolic and perceptual abilities, manifested in poor reading, much below the expected grade level for a particular age of the child" (Wagner 21). In addition, Wagner notes that a bill passed by Senator Yarborough of Texas, defines the learning disability as an inability to listen, write, spell, or do arithmetic (Wagner 19). T. R. Miles, Professor of Psychology at The University College of North Wales, adds in <u>The Dyslexic Child</u>, that correct reading is usually a minor problem, though a great deal . . . .

CONCLUSION OF THE RESEARCH PAPER

The conclusion is essential to your research paper. IT SHOULD BE, AT LEAST, A SUMMARY OF THE PAPER AND A RESTATEMENT OF THE THESIS STATEMENT. IF POSSIBLE, THE CONCLUSION SHOULD GO BEYOND A SUMMARY OR RESTATEMENT OF THE THESIS. For example, in an ARGUMENT RESEARCH PAPER, you should express with enthusiasm your particular side of the argument or discuss the validity of your findings in the essay. IN SHORT, YOU SHOULD SAY SOMETHING SIGNIFICANT THAT GOES BEYOND A MERE RESTATEMENT OF THE THESIS.

Here are some ways you can conclude your paper:

1. RESTATE THE THESIS, AND, IF POSSIBLE, GO BEYOND IT

Clearly, anorexia nervosa and bulimia are disorders which reflect our civilization's obsession with outward appearance. The very fact that victims cover a wide spectrum, from all ages and walks of life, illustrates how deeply this concept of thinness is imbedded in our society. Indeed, one cannot open a magazine or turn on the television without squarely confronting the issue; we are entrenched in the mire of narcissism. Certainly, society's attitudes must change before more young women become victims. Already, according to Current Health (10), two San Francisco hair salons have stopped using super skinny models in an effort to combat eating disorders. But that change is just a very small start. To stave off the ravages of eating disorders effectively, we must communicate respect for the person within the body—whatever that body might look like.

2. CONCLUDE WITH EFFECTIVE QUOTATIONS

Emma Bovary recognizes her own oppression and supports this writer's view when she says:

> A man is free, at least—free to range the passions and the world, to surmount obstacles, to taste the rarest pleasures. Whereas a woman is continually thwarted, inert, compliant, she has to struggle against her physical weakness and legal subjection. Her Will, like the veil tied to her hat, quivers with every breeze: there is always a desire that entices, always a convention that restrains (MB 101)

Period goes before the parenthesis in a long quotation.

But in the world that Flaubert creates, Emma gives up. Death, however, is no punishment; she has been punished by life (Nadeau 137). "And so," Nadeau concludes, "life takes her by the scruff of the neck and drowns her" (137).

3. SUMMARIZE THE PAPER'S POINTS—AND GO BEYOND BY REFERRING TO THE AUTHOR(S)

The age old taboo of incest has often caused the imagination of many to be creative. The central incestual character clash between Hippolytus and Phaedra has been dealt with in a myriad of interesting ways. As elucidated, in Euripides' Hippolytus, the action is directly attributed to the Gods, whereas in Racine's Phèdre, Hippolytus rejects his step-mother's affection because his heart belongs to another, that is, to Aricia. Lope de Vega introduces an enchanting variation in this relationship when he creates his Hippolytus and Phaedra as figures who are lusting for one another in Justice Without Revenge. Lastly, in Jeffers' The Cretan Women, Hippolytus, being a homosexual, naturally disclaims Phaedra's sexual advances.

Each of these writers has created three-dimensional human beings who shed light on incest, viewed in the past with fascination and alarm, and today, studied with renewed interest and perception. In today's society, incest is being reported more widely so that more and more studies are being conducted for a better understanding of this sexual phenomenon.

4. FOCUS THE CONCLUSION OF A LITERARY RESEARCH PAPER ON THE AUTHOR

Indeed, it is possible to demonstrate the link between Auto-da-Fe, the "Experimental Novel," and the Literature of the Absurd. However, it is quite obvious that Canetti's work cannot be simply nor easily categorized. On the contrary, this evaluation involves endless attempts to manipulate mentally the materials at hand, in order to draw conclusions and receive insights. Canetti's novel is the product of a highly complex mind, a mind that persists in its search for psychological reality as opposed to the actuality that most human beings experience in everyday existence.

5. CONCLUDE WITH ENTHUSIASM YOUR PLEA FOR THE POSITION YOU HAVE TAKEN IN AN ARGUMENT PAPER

Finally, now that both sides of this question have been explored, for or against the unity of Ireland, it is evident that if partition continues and the North and South remain separated, Ireland will lose its chance to obtain lasting peace, and the seeds of hatred and prejudice will continue to grow, feeding old injustices, real or imagined. Ireland's place in the modern world will be lost forever, and so will its chance to emerge in this century as one of the world's "Brightest and Newest Stars." And the brilliance that could have been will fade and be lost in the darkness of time.

FIFTH SESSION

In What Category Would You Place Your Research Paper?

PART TWO

Usually, research papers fall into three categories: ARGUMENTATION, ANALYSIS, AND EXPOSITION.

ARGUMENTATION

The argumentative, or critical research essay, interprets and argues an idea or issue. The author of such a research paper sets forth the problem, analyzing and explaining its complexities, takes a stand, and in so doing offers a solution, acknowledges opposing arguments and solutions, and restates, finally, his or her own stand or position as the best solution to the argument or problem. For example, the problem or question concerning karate as harmful, psychologically speaking, is a current subject under discussion by psychologists. Here is one possible way of handling this topic as an argumentative research essay:

I. INTRODUCTION: ANALYSIS OF THE PROBLEM
The student discusses and defines the problem of karate.

II. BODY: POSITION TAKEN BY THE WRITER OF THE PAPER
The student introduces evidence from authorities that suggest that karate may be harmful psychologically and takes a stand in that regard. This section may be several paragraphs long in presenting judgments about this position based upon research findings in PRIMARY and SECONDARY SOURCES, and opinions supported by the reference materials.

III. BODY: VERY BRIEF MENTION OF OPPOSING VIEWS OR SOLUTIONS
The student acknowledges arguments against his stand or point of view as developed in section II, but reasons that the evidence available against his position is inconclusive or invalid.

IV. CONCLUSION: AFFIRMATION OF ORIGINAL POSITION
Affirmation of original position developed in section II.

Some of the questions posed below, regarding psychology, and philosophy, suggest research papers of argumentation:

1. Is homosexuality abnormal?
2. Can psychosurgery be justified?
3. Do ESP and psychokinesis exist?
4. Are there valid arguments for sociobiology?
5. Does violence on TV cause aggressive behavior in children?
6. Should there be limits to genetic research?

7. What duties do human beings have to animals? Do animals have rights?
8. Can there be a "just" war in a nuclear age?
9. To what extent is it permissible to exploit the environment in order to expand industry and provide new jobs?
10. Should euthanasia of defective newborns be allowed?
11. How does one's beliefs in the value of human life, the worth of each person, one's common humanity and common dignity bear on the nature and methods of capital punishment as seen from a moral point of view?
12. How should a conflict of the right to life with the right to control one's own body be resolved?
13. Under what conditions, if any, is it ethical for psychiatrists to divulge information given to them in confidence?

INDUCTION AND DEDUCTION, AS METHODS OF REASONING, USEFUL IN <u>ARGUMENTATION</u>, WILL BE TREATED FURTHER ON IN RESEARCH AS EXPOSITION.

ANALYSIS

Some research paper topics fall into the category of analysis as the material presented requires the student to draw conclusions from the basic evidence, data, and facts which he or she has presented in the paper. For example, the purpose of one paper prepared for anthropology made an analysis of the archetypal images in the culture and politics of Nazi Germany, that is, an analysis of the component parts of these images, and reached interesting and valuable conclusions regarding the psychology of the Nazis' Third Reich. Another example concerns a careful, step-by-step analysis of the personality of August Strindberg, the famous Swedish playwright, and some of his important works such as <u>The Father</u> and <u>Miss Julie</u> and arrived at the conclusion that Strindberg, indeed, was a misogynist in both his life and art.

ANOTHER ASPECT OF ANALYSIS

If you were to write a research paper on the stages of hypnosis as a cure for the problem of obesity, your paper would involve what is called "Process Analysis." This process involves an explanation of the steps of an operation which lead to its conclusion. In one narrow view, process analysis may be considered narration, but process analysis has a different purpose than telling a story; process analysis explains methods that end in specified results such as a conclusion that might be reached showing how to make the United Nations more effective. Another example can be cited from chemistry: A Process Analysis of Carbon Dioxide in regard to Climate. Another example concerns "Freewriting": Its Importance as a Solution to Writing Problems.

ANALYSIS BY CHRONOLOGY

One may write a research paper which involves analysis by chronoloy, which has long been a standard procedure in organizing a research paper. Many subjects can be studied and developed by chronology. For example, in a history paper, one student wrote about the dress codes of the French Court of Louis XIV. The student explained that Louis XIV imposed strict dress codes for French nobles gradually, from styles of hair and hats, early in his reign, to the entire dress of a courtier as well as his social etiquette during the middle and end of his imperial influence. Thus, the King could control which nobles were favored. All apsects of the dress code required purchases, involving great sums of money, and only Louis's favorites were awarded royal annuities to make court appearances possible. Those whom the King disapproved of were kept penniless and therefore, they could not take part in the essential life of the French Court. (This chronological approach to this topic provides excellent organization of this research essay and provides a strong example of what is meant by Analysis by Chronology.)

Another example of a chronological approach comes from a literature paper on "The Evolution of Henrik Ibsen's Androgynous Woman: From Nora (1879) to Irene (1899)," a time span of Ibsen's gradual development in his own understanding of women. Since each female protagonist in this twenty-year time span in which Ibsen was writing, evolves into a fuller, more independent, more individualized "androgynous personality," the progression, through time, or by chronology, provides a further strong example of Analysis by Chronology.

EXPOSITION

Many research papers fall into the category of exposition, that is, essays which explain, inform, clarify, and define. This kind of research paper tends to be informative or informational rather than analytical. The purpose of this kind of paper is to gather facts and present and summarize data. Three types of expository research papers are those developed by CAUSE AND EFFECT, DEDUCTION AND INDUCTION, AND COMPARISON.

1. Cause and Effect

   Often, the effect (result or condition) is represented by the thesis sentence:

   Thomas Mann (1875–1955) employs Nietzsche's Apollonian/Dionysian dichotomy widely, in his novellas, particularly, Tonio Kröger and Death in Venice and in his major novel, The Magic Mountain. This general statement is an effect and the causes which substantiate this effect or result will be explored in the research essay by quoting some secondary sources as support and by quoting directly from the three primary sources by Mann mentioned in the thesis.

   Another example of cause and effect used in a research piece:

Thesis Sentence

Solzhenitsyn's novel Cancer Ward (1968) explores many areas of losses of human freedom in contemporary life in the Soviet Union.

This general statement is an effect and the causes or reasons which demonstrate that the effect is indeed true will be exposed in the research paper by quoting some secondary sources as support and by quoting directly examples of the losses of human freedom (loss of medical freedom, loss of educational freedom, loss of social, personal freedom, loss of political freedom, etc.) in Cancer Ward, the primary source.

A further example of cause and effect employed in a research paper:

Thesis Sentence

Most historians conclude now that Jefferson Davis, despite many failings, was a decided asset to the Confederacy.

This general statement is an effect (result or condition) and the causes (reasons) which will prove this conclusion will be cited from both primary and secondary sources in the research paper.

Another example:

Thesis Sentence

D. H. Lawrence (1885–1930) demonstrates the uses of touch as an act of major spiritual or psychological importance, beyond the mere physical action, in four short stories "Her Turn" (1912), "The Blind Man" (1914), "You Touched Me" (1917) and "Sun" (1924).

Again this general statement is an effect (result, condition, conclusion) and the causes (reasons) which substantiate this effect will be given from some secondary sources and in a great many examples quoted directly from the four stories, the four primary sources used in this paper.

2. Deduction and Induction

Another category concerns deduction and induction. Here two structures are involved either GENERAL TO SPECIFIC OR PARTICULAR (DEDUCTIVE), or PARTICULAR (SPECIFIC) TO GENERAL (INDUCTIVE). If you are going to present your material deductively, you must first formulate a general concept that you want to support with specific details and examples. For instance, a paper on alcoholism might begin with a general statement about the lifelong consequences of alcoholism. The entire paper would cite particulars and specifics to demonstrate the truth of the deductive generalizations.

Thesis Sentence

The results of alcoholism are far more destructive than was formerly known.
Specifics:

Physical problems
Marital complications
Filial dilemmas
Psychological problems
Societal strife

In another research piece, the student may wish to explore the specifics of the problem of alcoholism, inductively, before arriving at a conclusion. The student writing about alcoholism would present many case studies before he or she might be able to arrive at any conclusions. The writer would begin with specifics:

Case study #1
Case study #2
Case study #3
Case study #4, etc., etc., etc.

After studying the harmful effects as demonstrated by several case studies, the student writer may well be able to generalize at the end of his paper about the life-long, harmful effects of alcoholism. The writer's purpose is more to study specific case histories of alcoholism than to begin with the generalization (deduction) that alcoholism is life-threatening. The paper will be organized around the specifics and certain conclusions will probably follow at the end of the research essay.

3. Comparison and Contrast

Comparison and contrast exposition is one of the most common techniques of amplification. In more formal research papers, uses of comparison and contrast, should involve an ordered plan in order to keep the reader interested. Sometimes the purpose involves pointing out what the likeness and differences are, and in certain cases, to show the superiority of one thing or idea over another. One of the most important ways to arrange comparison and contrast is to present all the information on the two subjects, one at a time, and to summarize by combining their most important similarities and differences. Although expository comparisons and contrasts are often handled together, it is often best to present all the similarities first, then all the differences, or vice versa.

For example, a psychology paper uses comparison and contrast:

Thesis Sentence

A comparison of two aspects of the Dionysian, the creative and destructive, will be undertaken as seen in Nietzsche, Jung, and Moreno.

Another example, from sociology:

Thesis Sentence

The aim, therefore, of this paper is to compare anorexia nervosa with bulimia, two serious eating disorders which Western society induces by promoting the "ultra-thin ideal woman" image.

(The term comparison, or to compare, is most often used in an extended sense to indicate both comparison and contrast.)

Another example, from literature:

Thesis Sentence

This paper will compare and contrast the life styles revealed in the philosophies of the "Westernizer" and the "Slavophile" in Father and Sons (1862) by Ivan Turgenev (1818–1883) and The Cherry Orchard (1904) by Anton Chekhov (1860–1904).

A further example, from psychology:

Thesis Sentence

It is the intention of this paper to expose two main theorists of the century, Sigmund Freud (1856–1939) and Alfred Adler (1870–1937), and to compare their masculine viewpoints of feminine psychology.

FIFTH SESSION

Further Data on Preparing an Outline

PART THREE

You have three choices in regard to writing your outline for the research paper: TOPIC OUTLINE, SENTENCE OUTLINE, OR PARAGRAPH OUTLINE. You should use ONE FORM and not alternate forms within the outline. In the TOPIC OUTLINE FORM, every heading and sub-heading is involved with the use of a NOUN "Napoleon's Accomplishments as Hero of France," or its equivalent as a gerund phrase, "Accomplishing Cultural and Social Policies," or an infinitive phrase, "To Improve the Lot of the Jew in France." IN THE SENTENCE OUTLINE, HEADINGS AND SUB-HEADINGS ARE WRITTEN AS COMPLETE SENTENCES. WITH THE PARAGRAPH OUTLINE, EVERY SECTION IS A PARAGRAPH WITH MAJOR HEADINGS BEING WRITTEN AS NOUNS.

An outline shows the division of the ideas to be included in a paper, and because you cannot divide anything into only one part, numbers and letters in an outline must always appear at least in pairs. If you have an A, you must also have a B. If you use a 1, you must also use a 2, and so forth. You may, of course, have more than two subdivisions.

Here are the standard outline symbols:

I.

A.
1.
2.
a.
b.
(1)
(2)
(a)
(b)

B.
1.
2.
a.
b.
(1)
(2)
(a)
(b)

II.

A.

1.

2.

a.

b.

(1)

(2)

(a)

(b)

B.

1.

2.

a.

b.

(1)

(2)

(a)

(b)

III.

A.

B.

Method: Cause and Effect — Topic Outline

OUTLINE

Napoleon's Social and Cultural Accomplishments

Thesis: EFFECT — Aside from Napoleon's military accomplishments, he was considered from the time of his death and still today as one of France's greatest heroes owing to his important social and cultural legacies.

I. Increase in Popular Mémoires and Chronicles

- A. After death, (1821), increase in popular literature about Napoleon's greatness
- B. "Ode à la Colonne" by Victor Hugo, France's poet laureate
- C. Life of Napoleon: Emperor of the French. by Sir Walter Scott
- D. 200,000 volumes on Napoleon since 1900

II. Napoleon's Social and Cultural Policies

- A. The Concordat of 1801 re: Roman Catholicism in France
  1. Roman Catholicism as official religion of France
  2. Freedom of religion guaranteed for all Frenchmen (Catholic or not)
- B. New Civil Service Organization
  1. French Civil Servants and the State
  2. Bureaucratization
     - a. Military organization
     - b. Further characteristics
       - (1) Logic
       - (2) Rationality
       - (3) Inheritance from the Enlightenment
  3. New Divisions of France into Departments (Arrondisements and Communes): Broader responsibilities)
     - a. Public order
     - b. Health
     - c. Morality
  4. Influence throughout the world

C. Higher Education System of France
   1. Re-establishment of all French Universities (1808) (after abolishment of 1797)
   2. Primary of University of Paris: Enrollment one-third of all French youth
   3. Free education for college or university
      a. After high school graduation
      b. By examination

D. New ideas concerning Jews and Judaism in France
   1. Idea for establishment of Jewish State in Israel (1799)
   2. Meeting of Jewish notables
      a. Freedom of religion for Jews
      b. Protection of Jews as French citizens

E. Romanticism in painting
   1. Potent hold on artistic imagination in France
   2. Depiction of contemporary events: Glories of Napoleon's Empire
   3. Napoleon as God-like hero: inspiration of many painters (led by Jacques-Louis David and Theodore Géricault)

III. Napoleon today as Legendary and Mythological Hero

   A. Truth and fiction
   B. Rival of no Frenchman except, perhaps, St. Joan of Arc

Method: Cause and Effect

Sentence Outline

OUTLINE

Napoleon's Social and Cultural Accomplishments

Thesis: EFFECT — Aside from Napoleon's military accomplishment, he was considered from the time of his death, and still today, as one of France's greatest heroes owing to his important social and cultural legacies.

I. After Napoleon's death in 1821, there was a huge increase in the number of mémoires and chronicles extolling his greatness.

   A. Napoleon's legend was exploited in popular literature.

   B. Victor Hugo honored Napoleon by his "Ode à la Colonne" (1823).

   C. Sir Walter Scott published his Life of Napoleon Buonaparte. Emperor of the French (1825).

   D. Victoires et Conquêtes des Français, 28 volumes, was published (1828).

   E. Since the beginning of the 20th century, more than 200,000 volumes have been published on Napoleon and his times.

II. Napoleon's social and cultural policies were many years ahead of their time.

Method: Cause and Effect | Paragraph Outline

OUTLINE

Napoleon's Social and Cultural Accomplishments

Thesis: EFFECT — Aside from Napoleon's military accomplishments, he was considered from the time of his death, and still today, as one of France's greatest heroes owing to his important social and cultural legacies.

I. Increase in Popular Mémoires and Chronicles

A.–D. As soon as the Emperor was dead, the legend grew rapidly. Mémoires, notes, chronicles, and narratives by those who had followed him into exile contributed substantially to the hero worship in France. From 1821 until 1825, the number of books in Napoleon's honors increased continually: among them were Victor Hugo's "Ode à la Colonne," the 28 volumes of Victoires et Conquêtes des Français, and Sir Walter Scott's Life of Napoleon Buonaparte, Emperor of the French. Since the beginning of the 20th century, more than 200,000 volumes have been published on Napoleon and his times.

REMEMBER: YOU CANNOT WRITE A SUCCESSFUL RESEARCH PAPER WITHOUT FIRST WRITING AN OUTLINE BEFORE YOU BEGIN EVEN THE ROUGH DRAFT OF THE RESEARCH ESSAY.

OUTLINES ARE REQUIRED
FOR ALL RESEARCH PAPERS.

SIXTH SESSION

How to Use Internal Documentation Instead of Footnotes

Today, many academic departments in colleges, and many professional journals, are in the process of changing to a new style of documentation. This style, adopted in July 1984, has become the new official style of the Modern Language Association (MLA) and is already in use in its journal, Publication of the Modern Language Association, (PMLA). Footnotes or endnotes, once the method of documenting research sources, will no longer be the usual way of identifying and fully describing a source when it is first mentioned. INSTEAD, INTERNAL DOCUMENTATION, IN PLACE OF FOOTNOTES OR ENDNOTES, WILL BE USED IN THE TEXT OF THE RESEARCH PAPER.

For Example:

When you are quoting a book as a source (in a short quotation or a long quotation), use the author's name and provide a page number immediately after the quotation or paraphrase or immediately after the author's or authority's name.

Leslie A. Fiedler, a well-known critic of American literature, contends: "In the work of William Faulkner, the fear of a castrating woman and the dis-ease [sic] with sexuality . . . attain their fullest and shrillest expression (321).

Or

A distinguished literary authority, Leslie A. Fiedler (321) contends: "In the work of William Faulkner, etc., etc.

Or

If you do not mention the name of the author or authority in the text itself, include his or her name within parentheses along with the specific page number: For instance:

One expert on Faulkner explains that Vardaman Bundren in As I Lay Dying is not an idiot (Brooks 88).

THE SOURCE OF EVERY QUOTATION AND EVERY PARAPHRASE MUST BE CITED IN THE TEXT OF THE PAPER ITSELF

E. M. Forster expresses his partiality for Jane Austen by confessing: "I am a Jane Austenite, and therefore slightly imbecile about Jane Austen. . . . I read and re-read, the mouth open and the mind closed. I greet her by the name of the most kind hostess, while criticism slumbers" (148). Most readers of Mansfield Park, however, cannot so easily close their minds and allow criticism to slumber because this novel invites close scrutiny. The reader whose critical faculties are fully awake will discover that Austen, with consummate artistry, has woven elements of other literary genres into the fabric of the novel. One literary critic suggests that within literary scholarship, there is always room for a variety of points of view (Fleishman 26). Literature is, according to Northrop Frye, a most distinguished literary authority, "an inexhaustible source of new critical discoveries"(8). Mansfield Park (1813) is a novel that still invites new points of view. One of these is to consider the elements of drama, folklore, and myth.

"Lovers Vows" is the play Austen uses to emphasize moral aspects of the personalities in the novel. Although A Walton Litz notices that the drama in effect polarizes the moral attitudes of the novel, he does not observe that Austin employs the drama to accentuate her attitudes towards love and towards the society of her day (130). The motif of folklore Austen uses in the novel is that of the young and virtuous child mistreated by adults and siblings; the most familiar variant of this theme is Cinderella, the analogue of Fanny Price, the protagonist of Mansfield Park. The mythical motif is the archetypal theme of the rites of passage, particularly the hero's journey of separation, initiation, and return. Motifs are themes that are, as Vladimir Nabakov puts it, like the "images of an idea" repeated here and there in a novel much as a tune recurs in a fugue (16). In Mansfield Park, Austen repeats the tune of these motifs of drama, folklore, and myth to create a harmonious composition, whose counterpoint suggests that the essential ingredients for a reasonably happy and productive life are love and work.*

INCLUDE THE TITLE OF THE WORK WHENEVER NECESSARY FOR CLARITY

If you have used MORE THAN ONE BOOK OR WORK BY ONE AUTHOR, the use of his or her name with the appropriate page is NOT CORRECT PROCEDURE, SINCE IN THE "WORKS CITED," THERE WILL CONTAIN TWO REFERENCES TO THIS SAME AUTHOR. IN THIS CASE, YOU SHOULD INCLUDE THE TITLE OF THE WORK IN THE TEXT, AND, IF THE FULL TITLE SHOULD BE AN EXCEPTIONALLY LONG ONE, PROVIDE A SHORTENED VERSION OF THE TITLE. Here is an example:

"A woman who had been a schoolteacher married a coal miner, in the borough of Nottingham, two days after Christmas of 1875. She had never seen him dressed for the pits, and she knew nothing of the colliers' lives in the outlying villages" (Moore, The Priest of Love 3).

In the bleak Forties, when D. H. Lawrence was not widely appreciated and little read, Harry T. Moore suggested that Lawrence was "The Great Unread" and raised the battle flag "Why Not Read Lawrence, Too?" Moore believed that Lawrence should be read and insisted that Lawrence's works provide one of the most important and beautiful reading experiences in modern life (The Life and Works 2).

Complete titles of both the books cited above are The Priest of Love: A Life of D. H. Lawrence by Harry T. Moore and The Life and Works of D. H. Lawrence by Harry T. Moore. The two full titles, of course, will appear in "Works Cited" at the end of the paper itself.

*The above excerpt from a literary research paper is used with the permission of Dorothy Wylder, the author.

When dealing with one primary source, whether in literature (novels, short stories, poems, and drama are all primary sources), or in psychology (the original works of Freud, Jung, Adler, Erikson, and Piaget, et al., are primary sources), or any other primary sources, follow this practice.

Even though, in the case of a paper on Madame Bovary by Flaubert, the paper may be dealing with only one primary source, namely, Madame Bovary, it is a good idea to abbreviate the title Madame Bovary as (M.B.), a practice that avoids referring to Flaubert as the author of all the short and long quotations and paraphrase, a tedious repetition. In this connection, it is not necessary to write "On page 45 Flaubert tells the reader that . . . ." Rather, "Emma experiences deep disillusionment from her marriage. She cannot believe the deadening life she was leading" (M.B. 45). Madame Bovary may be abbreviated as MB, no periods needed.

This abbreviation of the title of the primary source should be also used in other fields such as psychology, sociology, anthropology, biology, philosophy, and others.

For example, in Psychology:

> Stanislov Grof traces psychology to the biological birth sequence (R.H.U. 44–153). The abbreviation R.H.U. stands for the complete title of Grof's book Realms of the Human Unconscious and may also be abbreviated as RHU, no periods necessary.
>
> Or
>
> Lloyd de Mause considers the interaction of fetus and placenta the basic psychological template ("F.O.H." 1–89). Here the primary source being cited is a long article which requires quotation marks round the title rather than underlining which is required for the titles of books and newspapers. The complete article abbreviated as "F.O.H." is "The Fetal Origins of History," in The Journal of Psychohistory. F.O.H. may also be abbreviated as "FOH," no periods necessary.
>
> Or
>
> R. D. Laing speculates on the influence that zygotal and embryological experience has on the structure of the human mind (F.L. 1–153). The full title here is Laing's The Facts of Life. (Also FL).

WHEN YOU ARE QUOTING OR PARAPHRASING AN ARTICLE RATHER THAN A BOOK, THE PROCEDURE IS EXACTLY THE SAME AS WAS FOLLOWED FOR THE INTERNAL DOCUMENTATION (INSTEAD OF FOOTNOTES) FOR A BOOK.

For Example:

> Lily Bart in The House of Mirth by Edith Wharton looks at herself and is, for the most part, viewed by the society she lives in as an object. In her provocative article, "The Temptation to Be a Beautiful Object: Double Standard and Double Bind in The House of Mirth," Judith Fetterley insists: "The tragedy of Lily Bart is peculiarly the tragedy of an upper class woman faced with 'the temptation to be a beautiful object,' which such a society presents to its women and she is destroyed by the consequences of that temptation" (4).
>
> Or
>
> One important Wharton critic insists: "The tragedy of Lily Bart is peculiarly the tragedy of an upper class woman . . ." (Fetterley 4).

WHEN YOU ARE QUOTING OR PARAPHRASING A NEWSPAPER ARTICLE, FOLLOW THE SAME PROCEDURE AS FOR A BOOK OR ARTICLE IN THAT YOU ALWAYS CITE THE NAME OF THE AUTHOR, SOMETIMES INCLUDING THE NAME OF THE BOOK OR ARTICLE, BUT NOT ALWAYS, AS THE TITLE WILL APPEAR IN THE "WORKS CITED." WITH A NEWSPAPER ARTICLE OR A POPULAR MAGAZINE ARTICLE THAT MIGHT BE UNSIGNED, YOU SHOULD ABBREVIATE THE TITLE OF THE NEWSPAPER ARTICLE ALONG WITH THE PAGE NUMBER. For example:

> The New York Times reports that "Jessye Norman celebrated her great success at the Metropolitan Opera's opening night Monday with Chinese food and an hour and a half of sleep" ("Jessye Norman . . ." B-1).

Or, a further example from a newspaper article:

> In a front page article of the New York Times of 12 Oct. 1984, a report comes from Stockholm: "Oct. 11—The Nobel Prize for Literature has been awarded to Jaroslav Seifert, a Czechoslovak poet, the Swedish Academy announced today" ("Jaroslav Seifert . . ." 1+).

IF YOU ARE QUOTING OR PARAPHRASING YOUR CLASS NOTES, YOU WILL REFER TO THEM AS AN ACADEMIC LECTURE BY PROFESSOR SO AND SO.
For instance:

> Furthermore, in several of his short stories, D. H. Lawrence uses the "Sleeping Beauty" motif, that is, the theme of awakening, in which the individual experiences a "discovery of the self" (Freeman 127). The word "Phoenix," differing from "Sleeping Beauty" was a favorite of Lawrence, and has also been used to describe this idea of awakening. In a talk in English 220: Honors Literature Seminar in the Forty-Seven Short Stories of Lawrence, Prof. Samuel Draper explained: "Whatever the vocabulary, all these terms refer to Lawrence's sense of movement from psychological death to psychological life, or 're-birth.' Laurence calls this human status before awakening as being 'dead-alive' " (Draper, lecture).

IF YOU ARE QUOTING OR PARAPHRASING WHAT IS REFERRED TO AS A COMPONENT PART OF A BOOK OR ARTICLE, PUT BOTH THE COMPONENT PART AND THE ORIGINAL SOURCE INTO THE WORKS CITED.

For example, you are reading The Priest of Love: A Life of D. H. Lawrence by Harry T. Moore, revised edition, published by Southern Illinois University Press, 1962. On page 353 of The Priest of Love, Moore quotes a literary critic of note, namely, Robert Lidell. Moore writes: "In the July 1954 issue of Essays in Criticism, Robert Lidell writes: 'Katherine Mansfield said somewhere that there were three Lawrences: the black devil, whom she hated; the prophet, in whom she did not believe; and the man and artist whom she loved and valued. Now that it is twenty-four years since he died, can we not rid ourselves of the devil and the prophet—for whom there is no future—and find the man and artist, who is immortal?' " (Lidell in Moore 353).

WORKS CITED

Lidell, Robert. "D. H. Lawrence." In The Priest of Love: A Life of D. H. Lawrence. By Harry T. Moore. Carbondale, IL: Southern Illinois UP, 1962, 353.

Moore, Harry T. The Priest of Love: A Life of D. H. Lawrence. Carbondale, IL: Southern Illinois UP, 1962.

Another example:

Hough, Graham. "Lawrence's Quarrel with Christianity: The Man Who Died." In D. H. Lawrence: A Collection of Critical Essays. Ed. Mark Spilka. Englewood Cliffs, NJ: Prentice, 1963, 101–111.

Spilka, Mark, ed. D. H. Lawrence: A Collection of Critical Essays. Englewood Cliffs, NJ: Prentice, 1963.

NOTE: Not only does the component part, that is, the smaller part of the whole, Robert Lidell and Graham Hough, is listed, but also the larger work, that is, Harry T. Moore and Mark Spilka, are included.

NOTE: For an in-text citation of these component parts write (Lidell in Moore with page in Moore) or (Hough in Spilka with page in Spilka).

SEVENTH SESSION

Format of the Research Paper and Some Mechanics of Writing MLA (Modern Language Association) Style Guide

Example of title page for MLA.

A Question of Idiocy: A Study of
Vardaman Bundren in William
Faulkner's *As I Lay Dying*

by

George Sheer

English 220: Honors Literature Seminar

Professor Libby Bay

Spring 1984

This paper has been prepared according to the new *Modern Language Association (MLA) Style Sheet* published in July 1984

Commercial thesis paper, with lined margins, is required.

This page is not numbered.

type title here

A Question of Idiocy: A Study of Vardaman Bundren in William Faulkner's As I Lay Dying

The mind of a young child is a wondrous, complex instrument. Its perceptual limits, which often far surpass those of adults, can often be quite perplexing, and ultimately mind-boggling. However, in some instances, the logic of a child is misinterpreted as a disorder, when in actuality, the child may be perfectly normal. Vardaman Bundren, in As I Lay Dying (1930) by William Faulkner (1897-1962), possesses these labyrinthine inner thoughts, which can ultimately lead the unobservant reader astray

. . . .

. . . .

. . . .

. . . .

First page of the text

Start pagination here on page 2 → 2

Though this quandary is emotionally baffling, the term "idiot" is not warranted.

Jean Piaget, a noted French developmental psychologist, refers to this childhood predicament as the adaption process of assimilation and accommodation (Piaget 228).

. . . .

. . . .

. . .

. . . .

Works Cited follows, on a separate page, the end of the text.

An example of the form of a short works cited...

Works Cited

Adams, Richard P. Faulkner: Myth and Motion. Princeton, NJ: Princeton UP, 1973.

Barth, J. Robert. Religious Perspectives in Faulkner's Fiction. Notre Dame, IN: U Notre Dame P, 1972.

Bee, Helen. The Developing Child. 3rd ed. New York: Harper, 1981.

Brooks, Cleanth. William Faulkner: First Encounters. New Haven and London: Yale UP, 1963.

ABBREVIATIONS

Abbreviations are generally used in the list of Works Cited but seldom in the text of the research paper itself. If the abbreviation is used in the text, it is generally used within parentheses.

When abbreviating, always use commonly accepted forms. In appropriate places, you may abbreviate days, months, and other measurements of time, states and countries, reference words common in scholarship, and publishers names.

The trend today in abbreviation is to use neither periods after letters nor spaces between letters: *Examples:* BC (Before Christ), NY (New York), PhD (Doctor of Philosophy).

Exception:

T. S. Eliot

The exception to this new trend continues to be the initials used for personal names. A period and a space follow each initial.

Abbreviations of Time

AD	*anno Domini* (in the year of the Lord); used before numerals: AD 380
a.m.	*ante meridiem* (before noon)
Apr.	April
Aug.	August
BC	before Christ; used after numerals: 20 BC
Dec.	December
Feb.	February
Fri.	Friday
hr., hrs.	hour, hours
Jan.	January
Mar.	March
mo., mos.	month, months
Mon.	Monday
Nov.	November
Oct.	October
p.m.	post meridiem (after noon)
Sat.	Saturday
Sept.	September
Sun.	Sunday
Thurs.	Thursday
Tues.	Tuesday
Wed.	Wednesday
wk., wks.	week, weeks
yr., yrs.	year, years

The months May, June, and July should not be abbreviated.

Geographical Names

You should spell out names of states, territories, territories of the United States and all the names of all countries in the text of the research paper with a few exceptions, for example, USSR, BRD (West Germany) and DDR (East Germany). In documentation of Works Cited, abbreviate the names of states, provinces, and countries (use a standard dictionary for these purposes).

Abbreviations of the Individual States of the United States Used by The U.S. Postal System, Acceptable to the MLA

AL	Alabama	MT	Montana
AK	Alaska	NB	Nebraska
AZ	Arizona	NV	Nevada
AR	Arkansas	NH	New Hampshire
CA	California	NJ	New Jersey
CO	Colorado	NM	New Mexico
CT	Connecticut	NY	New York
DE	Delaware	NC	North Carolina
DC	District of Columbia	ND	North Dakota
FL	Florida	OH	Ohio
GA	Georgia	OK	Oklahoma
GU	Guam	OR	Oregon
HI	Hawaii	PA	Pennsylvania
ID	Idaho	PR	Puerto Rico
IL	Illinois	RI	Rhode Island
IN	Indiana	SC	South Carolina
IA	Iowa	SD	South Dakota
KS	Kansas	TN	Tennessee
KY	Kentucky	TX	Texas
LA	Louisiana	UT	Utah
ME	Maine	VT	Vermont
MD	Maryland	VI	Virgin Islands
MA	Massachusetts	VA	Virginia
MI	Michigan	WA	Washington
MN	Minnesota	WV	West Virginia
MS	Mississippi	WI	Wisconsin
MO	Missouri	WY	Wyoming

Some Shortened Forms of Publishers' Names

Abrams	Harry N. Abrams, Inc.
Allen	George Allen and Unwin Publishers, Inc.
Allyn	Allyn and Bacon, Inc.
Appleton	Appleton-Century-Crofts
Ballantine	Ballantine Books, Inc.
Bantam	Bantam Books, Inc.
Barnes	Barnes and Noble Books
Basic	Basic Books
Beacon	Beacon Press, Inc.
Bobbs	The Bobbs-Merrill Co., Inc.
Bowker	R. R. Bowker Co.
Cambridge UP	Cambridge University Press
Clarendon	Clarendon Press
Columbia UP	Columbia University Press
Cornell UP	Cornell University Press

Dell	Dell Publishing Co., Inc.
Dodd	Dodd, Mead, and Co.
Doubleday	Doubleday and Co., Inc.
Dover	Dover Publications, Inc.
Dutton	E. P. Dutton, Inc.
Farrar	Farrar, Straus, and Giroux, Inc.
Free	The Free Press
Funk	Funk and Wagnalls, Inc.
Gale	Gale Research Co.
GPO	Government Printing Office
Harcourt	Harcourt Brace Jovanovich, Inc.
Harper	Harper and Row Publishers, Inc.
Harvard Law Rev. Assn.	Harvard Law Review Association
Harvard UP	Harvard University Press
Heath	D. C. Heath and Co.
Holt	Holt, Rinehart, and Winston, Inc.
Houghton	Houghton Mifflin Co.
Indiana UP	Indiana University Press
Johns Hopkins UP	The Johns Hopkins University Press
Knopf	Alfred A. Knopf, Inc.
Lippincott	J. B. Lippincott Co.
Little	Little, Brown, and Co.
Macmillan	Macmillan Publishing Co.
McGraw	McGraw-Hill, Inc.
MLA	The Modern Language Association of America
NAL	The New American Library, Inc.
NCTE	The National Council of Teachers of English
NEA	The National Education Association
Norton	W. W. Norton and Co., Inc.
Oxford	Oxford University Press
Penguin	Penguin Books, Inc.
Pocket	Pocket Books
Prentice	Prentice-Hall, Inc.
Princeton UP	Princeton University Press
Putnam's	G. P. Putnam's Sons
Rand	Rand McNally and Co.
Random	Random House, Inc.
St. Martin's	St. Martin's Press, Inc.
Scott	Scott, Foresman, and Co.
State U of New York P	State University of New York Press
U of California P	University of California Press
U of Chicago P	University of Chicago Press
U of Toronto P	University of Toronto Press
UP of Florida	University Presses of Florida
Viking	The Viking Press, Inc.
Yale UP	Yale University Press

THE USE OF TITLES IN THE RESEARCH PAPER

According to the MLA Handbook for Writers of Research Papers (1984), "The rules for capitalizing titles are strict. In both titles and subtitles, capitalize the first words, the last words, and all principal words." One must capitalize nouns, pronouns, verbs, adjectives, and adverbs, but not articles (a, an, the), prepositions (in, to, by, of), coordinating conjunctions (and, or, for, but, yet, nor), or to in infinitives, when such words come in the middle of the title.

For example, in titles of books which are underlined:

The Intelligent Heart: The Story of D. H. Lawrence
The Life of the Drama
What Is Literature?
Modern Essays on Writing and Style

Or

For example, in titles of articles or poems which are put in quotations:

"How a Child's Pretend World Can Be Helpful in the Real World" (article)
"A Narrow Fellow in the Grass" (poem)
"There's a Certain Slant of Light" (poem)

TITLES WHICH SHOULD BE UNDERLINED

Titles to be underlined include the names of BOOKS, PLAYS, LONG POEMS PUBLISHED AS BOOKS, PAMPHLETS, PERIODICALS (NEWSPAPERS, MAGAZINES, AND SCHOLARLY JOURNALS), FILMS, RADIO AND TV PROGRAMS, RECORD ALBUMS, BALLETS, OPERAS, MUSICAL COMPOSITIONS, PAINTINGS, WORKS OF SCULPTURE, SHIPS, AIRCRAFT, AND SPACECRAFT.

In these examples, you will notice that the underlining is NOT BROKEN BETWEEN WORDS.

Sons and Lovers (published book)
Hamlet (long play)
The Four Quartets (long poem)
Hello! I Am the Chow Chow (pamphlet)
Los Angeles Times (newspaper); do not capitalize the Los Angeles Times with a capital The.
Life (magazine)
Modern Drama (periodical)
D. H. Lawrence Review (scholarly journal)
The Bostonians (film)
Life from Lincoln Center (television program)
Bentley on Brecht (record album)
Swan Lake (ballet)
Tristan und Isolde (opera)
Moussorgsky's Pictures at an Exhibition (instrumental musical composition identified by name)
Manet's Picnic on the Grass (painting)
Praxiteles's Hermes and the Infant Dionysus (sculpture)
HMS Elizabeth II (ship)
Spirit of St. Louis (airplane)

TITLES IN QUOTATION MARKS

You should enclose in quotation marks, and DO NOT UNDERLINE, the titles of articles, essays, short stories, short plays, short poems, chapters of books, and individual episodes of radio and television programs, arias from operas, that is, all works that appear within larger works. Also use quotation marks for songs and unpublished works, such as lectures and speeches.

"An American Soprano Adds the Met to Her Roster" (newspaper article)
"Tanzania: At Large in East Africa" (article in a magazine)
"Michel de Ghelderode: A Personal Statement" (article in a scholarly journal)
"Irish Music" (encyclopedia article)
"How Should One Read a Book?" (essay in a book)
"The Rocking Horse Winner" (short story)
"The Black and White" (short play)
"We Are Transmitters" (short poem)
"God Bless America" (song)
"Liebestod" (aria from Tristan und Isolde, opera)
"Techniques of Satire" (chapter from a book)
"Death and Rebirth in the Short Stories of D. H. Lawrence" (lecture)

EXCEPTIONS TO THE RULE OF UNDERLINING AND QUOTATIONS

Sacred Writings

Bible, King James Version, Old Testament, Genesis, Gospels, Talmud, Koran, Upanishads

Series

Bollingen Series
The University of California Studies in Comparative Literature

Societies

The American Friends of Michel de Ghelderode
Renaissance Society of America

Descriptive Words of Phrases

George Washington's first inaugural address

Courses

English 220–221: Honors Literature Seminar in War and Peace by Tolstoy
Honors Calculus 203–204

Divisions within a Book

preface, introduction, bibliography, appendix, chapter 2; act 4, scene 10, stanza 402, canto 102.

EIGHTH SESSION

Preparation of the Works Cited Section

Usually, you should alphabetize entries in the list of works cited by the author's last name, or if the author's name is unknown, by the first word in the title except for *A, An,* or *The*. For example, in an unsigned newspaper article "A Star is Born in Morristown," one would alphabetize this piece under "S."

GENERAL GUIDELINES FOR CITING BOOKS

According to the MLA Handbook, "an entry in a list of works cited characteristically has three main divisions—author, title, and publication information—each followed by a period and two spaces, not one space."

Biancolli, Louis. The Flagstad Manuscript. New York: Putnam's, 1952.

From time to time, other facts are required, and a period and two spaces (*not one*) follow each additional item of information.

Cather, Willa. "Paul's Case." In Literature: Structure, Sound and Sense. By Laurence Perrine. With the assistance of Thomas R. Arp. 4th ed. New York: Harcourt, 1983. 176–190.

According to the MLA, in citing books, normally arrange the information in the following order:

1. Author's name
2. Title of the part or component part of the book
3. Title of the book.
4. Name of the editor, translator, or compiler
5. Edition used
6. Number of volumes
7. Name of the series
8. Place of publication, that is, the city of publication (and an abbreviation of the state if the city is small and relatively unknown), name of the publisher, and date of publication
9. Page numbers

SAMPLE ENTRIES: BOOKS

A BOOK BY ONE AUTHOR

Donaldson, Scott. Fool for Love: F. Scott Fitzgerald. New York: Congdon, 1983.

Eliot, T[homas] S[tearns]. The Cocktail Party: A Comedy. New York: Harcourt, 1950.

Stassinopoulos, Arianna. Maria Callas: The Woman behind the Legend. New York: Simon, 1981.

AN ANTHOLOGY BY ONE AUTHOR

Decker, Randall E. Patterns of Exposition 7. Boston: Little, 1982.

TWO OR MORE BOOKS BY THE SAME AUTHOR

In citing two or more books by the same author, give the name of the author in the first entry only. Thereafter, in place of the name, type three hyphens and a period, skip two spaces, and give the title. The three hyphens always stand for exactly the same name(s) as in the preceding entry. If the person named served as editor, translator, or compiler of any of the books, place a comma (not a period) after the three hyphens, skip a space, and write the appropriate abbreviation (ed., trans., or comp.) before the title. Works listed under the same name(s) are alphabetized by title.

Bentley, Eric Russell. Are You Now or Have You Ever Been? New York: New Republic, 1977.
---. Bernard Shaw. New York: New Directions, 1957.
---. In Search of Theatre. New York: Vintage, 1954.
---. Life of the Drama. New York: Atheneum, 1964.
Frye, Northrop. Anatomy of Criticism: Four Essays. Princeton: Princeton UP, 1957.
---, ed. Sound and Poetry. New York: Columbia UP, 1957.

ONE BOOK BY TWO OR MORE AUTHORS

In citing a book by two or more persons, give their names in the order in which they appear on the title page—not necessarily in alphabetical order. Reverse only the name of the first author, and give the other name(s) in normal order: Kennedy, X. J. and Dorothy M. Kennedy. Place a period after the last name, skip two spaces and begin the next item of the entry. If there are more than three authors, name only the first and add "et al." ("and others"). If the persons listed on the title page are editors, translators, or compilers, place a comma (not a period) after the last name and add the appropriate abbreviation (eds., trans., or comp.).

Druckman, Daniel, Richard M. Rozelle, and James C. Baxter. Non-verbal Communication: Survey, Theory, and Research. Beverly Hills, CA: Sage, 1982.
Edens, Walter, et al., eds. Teaching Shakespeare. Princeton: Princeton UP, 1977.
Eisdorfer, C., et al. Models for Clinical Psychopathology. New York: Spectrum, 1984.
Spiller, Robert E., et al. Literary History of the United States. New York: Macmillan, 1960.

TWO OR MORE BOOKS BY THE SAME MULTIPLE AUTHORS

In citing two or more works by the same multiple authors, give the names of the authors in the first entry only. Thereafter, in place of the names, type three hyphens, followed by a period; skip two spaces, and give the next title. The three hyphens always stand for exactly the same name(s) as in the preceding entry.

Eisdorfer, Carl and William F. Farnsworth. Treatment of Psychopathology in the Aging. New York: Springer, 1982.
---. Handbook of Abnormal Psychology. New York: Edits, 1973.

A BOOK BY A CORPORATE AUTHOR

Cite the book by the corporate author, even if the corporate author is the publisher.

American Association of the Community and Junior Colleges. Community and Junior Colleges and the Comprehensive Employment and Training Act: Participation and Recommendations for Improvement. Washington: American Association of Community and Juniors Colleges, 1977.

AN ANONYMOUS BOOK

If a book has no author's name on the title page, do not use either "Anonymous" or "Anon." Begin the entry with the title and alphabetize by the first word other than a definite or indefinite article. Notice in the examples below that The Simon and Schuster Book of the Opera: A Complete Reference Guide: 1597 to the Present is alphabetized under "S" for Simon.

Dictionary of Geological Terms. New York: Anchor, 1976.
Handbook on the People's China. New York: AMS, 1974.
The Simon and Schuster Book of the Opera: A Complete Reference Guide: 1597 to the Present. New York: Simon, 1977.

A WORK IN AN ANTHOLOGY

You should state the author, first, and then the title of the piece you are citing (an essay or article, a short story, a drama, or a poem) enclosing the title in quotation marks but underlining if the work was originally published as a book. If the anthology contains works by different translators, give the translator's name preceded by the abbreviation "Trans." and followed by the title of the anthology which is underlined.

O'Connor, Flannery. "Everything That Rises Must Converge." In Interpreting Literature: Preliminaries to Literary Judgment. Eds. K. L. Knickerbocker and H. Willard Reninger. 6th ed. New York: Holt, 1978. 120–134.
Garcia Marquez, Gabriel. "A Very Old Man with Enormous Wings." "Leaf Storm" and Other Stories. Trans. Gregory Rebassa. New York: Harper, 1972. 105–112.

AN INTRODUCTION, PREFACE, FOREWORD, OR AFTERWORD

To cite an introduction, preface, foreword, or afterword, begin with the name of its author and then give the name of the part being cited, capitalized but neither underlined nor put in quotation marks (Introduction, Preface, Foreword, Afterword). If the writer of the smaller part you are quoting is different from the author of the complete work, cite the author of the larger work after the title of the larger work. Give the full name of the author in normal order, preceded by the word "By."

Flagstad, Kirsten. Preface. The Flagstad Manuscript. By Louis Biancolli. New York: Putnam's, 1952.
Garson, Kanin. Introduction. A Knight at the Opera: Sir Rudolf Bing. By Sir Rudolf Bing. New York: Putnam's, 1981.

A COMPONENT PART OR SMALLER PART OF A BOOK

You should follow the directions above for an introduction, preface, foreword, etc.: The author of the smaller part of the larger book comes first, and then the title of the piece you are citing (or quoting or paraphrasing in the text of the paper) enclosing the title in quotation marks if the component part is an essay, article, short story, short play, or a short poem but underlining if the work was originally published as a book.

Fitzgerald, F. Scott. "College Humor." In Scott Fitzgerald: A Biography. By Andrew Turnbull. New York: Ballantine, 1971.

Snodgrass, W. D. "A Rocking Horse: The Symbol, The Pattern, The Way to Live." In D. H. Lawrence: A Collection of Critical Essays. Ed. Mark Spilka. Englewood Cliffs, NJ: Prentice, 1963.

Trilling, Lionel. "Willa Cather." In Willa Cather and Her Critics. Ed. James Schroeter. Ithaca, NY: Cornell UP, 1967.

A TRANSLATION: TEXT RATHER THAN TRANSLATOR'S WORK IS UNDER DISCUSSION

Ghelderode, Michel de. The Strange Rider and Seven Other Plays by Michel de Ghelderode. Trans. Samuel Draper. New York: Curtis Brown, 1964.

A TRANSLATION: TRANSLATOR'S WORK RATHER THAN TEXT IS UNDER DISCUSSION

Draper, Samuel, trans. The Strange Rider and Seven Other Plays by Michel de Ghelderode. New York: Curtis Brown, 1964.

A REPUBLISHED BOOK

In citing a republished book, for instance, a paperback version of a book originally published in a clothbound version, give the date of publication of the original version, followed by a period and two spaces (not one), before the publication information for the book you are citing.

Biancolli, Louis. The Flagstad Manuscript. 1952. New York: Arno, 1977.

Doctorow, E. L. Welcome to Hard Times. 1960. New York: Bantam, 1976.

AN ARTICLE IN AN ENCYCLOPEDIA, DICTIONARY OR REFERENCE BOOK

An encyclopedia article or dictionary entry should be treated as a piece in a collection or anthology or as a component part of the whole. If the encyclopedia arranges articles alphabetically, you may omit volume and page numbers. When citing familiar reference books, especially those that frequently appear in new editions, the Encyclopaedia Britannica, for example, do not give full publication information. For such works, list only the edition (if stated) and the year of publication. When dealing with less familiar works such as the Dictionary of Mythology: Mainly Classical, give full publication information.

"Flamboyant Gothic Style." Encyclopaedia Britannica: Micropaedia. 1974 ed.

"Flaubert, Gustave." Encyclopaedia Britannica: Micropaedia. 1974 ed.

Evans, Bergen. "Athena." Dictionary of Mythology: Mainly Classical. Lincoln, NE: Centennial, 1970.

Fleischmann, Aloys. "Irish Music." Encyclopedia Americana, 1966.

GOVERNMENT PUBLICATIONS

If the author of the government publication is not known, treat the government as the author. State the name of the government first, followed by the name of the agency, using an abbreviation if the context makes the abbreviation clear. If you are citing more than one work by the same government agency, substitute three hyphens for the name in each entry after the first. The title of the publication, underlined, should follow the data given above. In citing a congressional document other than the Congressional Record (which requires only a date and a page number), include such information as the number and session of Congress, the House (HR) or Senate (S) and the type and number of the publication. Types of congressional publications include bills (S33; HR 77), resolutions (S. Res. 20; H. Res. 50), reports (S. Rept. 9; H. Doc. 222). The usual publication information comes next that is, place, publishers, and the date. Most federal publications, regardless of the branch of government, are published by the Government Printing Office (GPO) in Washington, D.C. Documents issued by the United Nations and most local governments, however, do not issue from Washington or any other central office; in this case, give the publishing information that appears on the title page.

New York State. Committee on State Prisons. Investigation of the New York State Prisons. 1883. New York: Arno, 1974.

United States. Cong. Hearing before a Subcommittee of the Committee on Government Operations: House of Representatives: Safety and Offshore Oil. 97th Cong., 2nd session (June 2, 1982). Washington: GPO, 1983.

---. U.S. Department of Justice. National Institute of Law Enforcement and Criminal Justice: Law Enforcement Assistance Adm. Gambling Law Enforcement in Major American Cities: Executive Summary. Washington: GPO, 1978.

Reiff, Robert, Ph.D. and Frank Riessman, Ph.D. The Indigenous Non-professional: A Strategy of Change in Community Action and Community Mental Health Programs. Washington, National Institute of Mental Health, 1982.

A BOOK PUBLISHED BEFORE 1900

When citing a book published before 1900, you may omit the name of the publisher.

Cole, David. History of Rockland County, N.Y. with Biographical Sketches of Its Prominent Men. 1884.

A BOOK WITHOUT STATED PUBLICATION DATA OR PAGINATION

When a book does not include the publisher, the place or date of publication, or the pagination, supply as much of the missing data as you can, enclosing such information in brackets to show that it did not come from the original source.

New York: Knickerbocher, [1972].

If the date can only be approximated, put it after a "c." for "circa" meaning "around." For example [c. 1835]. If you cannot supply any information, use the following abbreviations:

n.p.	no place of publication given
n.p.	no publisher given
n.d.	no date of publication given
n.pag.	no pagination given

Inserted before the colon, the abbreviation "n.p." indicates "no place"; after the colon it indicates "no publisher." "N. pag." informs your reader why no page references for the work are included in your citations.

No Date

New York: Knickerbocher, n.d.

No Pagination

New York: Knickerbocher, 1972. No pag.

No place

N.p.: Knickerbocher, 1972.

No Publisher

New York: n.p. 1972.

Neither Place nor Publisher

N.P.: n.p., 1972.
The Dog in Folk Art around the World. France: n.p., n.d. [Pagination included].

UNPUBLISHED DISSERTATION

Worby, Diana. "Objective and Subjective Modes of Alienation." Master's Essay. Manhattanville College, 1975.

PUBLISHED DISSERTATION

Rosenthal, Marilyn. Poetry of the Spanish Civil War. Diss. New York U, 1972. Berkeley, CA: U of California P, 1974.

A PAMPHLET

Treat a pamphlet as you would a book.

Thompson, Lawrance. Robert Frost. Minneapolis: U of Minnesota P.

GENERAL GUIDELINES FOR CITING PERIODICALS (magazines, journals, reviews)

According to the MLA Handbook, "an entry for an article in a periodical, like an entry for a book, has three main divisions: author, title of the article, and publication information. For scholarly journals, publication information generally includes the journal title, volume number, the year of publication, and inclusive page numbers."

Draper, Samuel. "Michel de Ghelderode: A Personal Statement." Tulane Drama Review 8.1 (1963): 33–38.

Sometimes, however, additional information is required. In citing articles in periodicals, normally arrange the information in the following order:

1. Author's name
2. Title of the article
3. Name of the periodical
4. Series number or name
5. Volume number
6. Date of publication
7. Page numbers

Regarding date of publication, leave a space after the volume number and give the year of the publication, in parentheses, followed by a colon, one space, and the inclusive page numbers in the article:

Modern Age 28 (Spring 1971): 714–720.

SAMPLE ENTRIES: ARTICLES

Regarding page numbers, give the pages for the complete article, not just the pages used. When an article is not printed on consecutive pages—if, for example, it begins on page 6, then skips to page 12, and continues on page 23 and 24—write only the first page number and a plus sign, leaving no intervening space, for example:

Kolodin, Irving. "The Young Old Bolshoi Opera." Saturday Review 9 Aug. 1975:52+.

SAMPLE ENTRIES: ARTICLES IN PERIODICALS

Regarding an article in a journal with continuous pagination, that is, the first issue ends on page 101, the next one begins on 102, give the volume number followed by the year of publication (in parentheses), a colon, and the inclusive page numbers.

AN ARTICLE IN A JOURNAL WITH CONTINUOUS PAGINATION

Armstrong, Gregory K. "Life after Study Abroad: A Survey of Undergraduate Academic and Career Choices." The Modern Language Journal 68.1 (1984): 1–4.

Benseler, David P. "Doctoral Degrees Granted in Foreign Language Study in the United States." The Modern Language Journal 68.3 (1984): 241–257.

Martin, Marilyn. "Advanced Vocabulary Teaching: The Problem of Synonyms." The Modern Language Journal 68.2 (1984): 130–137.

AN ARTICLE IN A JOURNAL THAT PAGES EACH ISSUE SEPARATELY OR THAT ONLY USES ISSUE NUMBERS

For a journal that does not number pages continuously throughout an annual volume but begins each issue on page 1, add a period and the issue number, without any intervening space, right after the volume number (for example, 12.2, signifying volume 12 issue 2; 8.1–2, for volume 8, issue 1 and 2 combined).

Suckow, Ruth. "Modern Figures of Destiny: D. H. Lawrence and Frieda Lawrence." In The D.H.Lawrence Review 31.1 (1970): 25-31.

AN ARTICLE FROM A WEEKLY OR BIWEEKLY PERIODICAL

Swan, Annalyn. "Montreal's Wonder Worker: Charles Dutoit." Newsweek 22 Oct. 1984: 95.

Walsh, Michael. "Champagne Time for Beverly Sills: City Opera's Ex-Diva Restores It to Vitality and Prominence." Time 29 Oct. 1984: 104.

AN ARTICLE FROM A MONTHLY OR BIMONTHLY PERIODICAL

Dunham, Bob. "The Curse of the Writing Class: Why Are So Many Writers Alcoholics?" Saturday Review Feb. 1984: 26–30.

AN ARTICLE FROM A DAILY NEWSPAPER

In citing a daily newspaper, give the name as it appears on the masthead but omit the introductory article: Los Angeles Times (not The Los Angeles Times). If the city of publication is not included in the name of the newspaper, add it in square brackets, not underlined, after the name: Journal-News [West Nyack, NY]. Next, give the complete date—day, month (abbreviated) and year. Because different editions of newspapers contain different material, specify the edition (if one is given on the masthead), preceded by a comma, after the date.

Molotsky, Irvin. "New Head of Smithsonian Installed." New York Times 18 Sept. 1984, late ed.,: C19, Col.3.

Mydans, Seth. "20 Years Later, Khrushchev Is Dim Memory for Russians" New York Times 15 Oct. 1984, early ed.: 1+

And for the Sunday New York Times, which organizes the Sunday edition according to sections 1 through 10, write the section number after the edition identification.

Rockwell, John. "Solti's 1959 'Rheingold' Wears Well in Its CD Incarnation." New York Times 28 Oct. 1984, late ed., sec. 2: 25, Col. 4.

Walsh, James. "Evidence from Search Can't Be Used in Trial." Journal-News [West Nyack, NY] 28 June 1984: B1.

If there is no author to cite in newspaper articles, alphabetize the entry under the first word of the title:

"Gribetz Expected to Take Leadership of State D.A.s." Journal-News [West Nyack, NY] 28 June 1984: B3.

(The above entry is alphabetized under "G.")

CLASS NOTES OR LECTURES: OTHER LECTURES, SPEECHES, AND ADDRESSES

Bay, Libby. "Faulkner's Yoknapatawpha Country." Lecture presented in English 221: Honors Literature Seminar in Faulkner, Rockland Community College, 16 Feb. 1984.

Ridley, Florence. "Forget the Past, Reject the Future: Chaos Is Come Again." Div. on Teaching of Literature, MLA Convention, Los Angeles, 28 Dec. 1982.

RADIO PROGRAMS

Les Troyens (The Trojans). By Hector Berlioz. With Jessye Norman and Placido Domingo. Cond. James Levine. Metropolitan Opera. Texaco-Metropolitan Opera Radio Network. WQXR, New York, NY. 18 Feb. 1984.

TELEVISION PROGRAMS

Lincoln Center Special. "Twenty-Fifth Anniversary of Lincoln Center for the Performing Arts." Clips from past broadcasts of all the participating organizations in Lincoln Center, New York City. PBS, WNET, Channel 13, Newark. 26 Oct. 1984.

INTERVIEWS

There are many different kinds of interviews, published or recorded interviews, interviews conducted by the researcher or writer of the research paper, interviews on television and radio, among others. The first entry should be that of the person who has been interviewed. If the interview is a part of a publication, recording, or program, put the title in quotation marks. If the interview is the entire work, underline the title. If the interview is untitled, use the descriptive "Interview." without underlining it nor enclosing it in quotation marks. Interviewers' names may be included if known and if they are pertinent.

Ghelderode, Michel de. Interview with the distinguished Belgian playwright. Brussels, Belgium, 10 April 1960. With Samuel Draper.

Herman, Robert. Interview about Maria Callas. Metropolitan Opera House, New York City, NY, 12 Dec. 1963.

Norman, Jessye. "Interview after Metropolitan Debut: 26 Sept. 1984." "Today Show," NBC 27 Sept. 1984. With Jane Paulee.

Stravinsky, Igor. Conversation with Igor Stravinsky. With Robert Craft. Berkeley: U of California P, 1980.

In citing a personally conducted interview, give the name of the interviewee, the kind of interview, and the date.

Bing, Rudolph. Personal interview. 10 Jan. 1966.

Miller, Gunhild. Telephone interview. 25 Sept. 1984.

LETTERS

Brawne, Fanny. "To Fanny Keats." 25 Dec. 1820. Letters from Fanny Brawne to Fanny Keats: 1820–1824. Ed. Fred Edgcumbe. New York: Oxford UP, 1937.

Flagstad, Kirsten. Letter to the author. 10 Sept. 1949.

LIMITED USE OF TRADITIONAL FOOTNOTES OR ENDNOTES IN THE NEW MLA STYLE:

CONTENT ENDNOTES

An endnote may be used which does not supply documentation of sources. CONTENT ENDNOTES ARE NOT DOCUMENTATION NOTES. In the new MLA system of documentation, references to sources are now made by in-text citation and the full entries are written in "Works Cited."

Content endnotes will seldom be used in undergraduate research.

A content endnote may contain data, explanations, interpretations, translations, and definitions which would be perhaps intrusive in the text of the paper itself.

If you do use endnotes, place them on a separate page following the last page of the text. Label the page "Notes."

For example, in a research paper on Ralph Waldo Emerson, the student writes as follows:

"Emerson belonged to a group called the 'New England Transcendentalists.'[8] Whether this coterie of intellectuals had. . . ."

Notes

[8]New England Transcendentalists. A group of writers and philosophers who were loosely bound together by adherence to an idealistic system of thought based on a belief in the essential unity of all creation, the innate goodness of man, the supremacy of insight over logic and experience for the revelation of the deepest truths. (This definition comes from the Encyclopaedia Britannica, Micropaedia, 1974, listed under "Transcendentalists, New England.")

NINTH SESSION

APA (American Psychological Association) Style Guide

The APA method of documentation and citing sources is very close to the MLA (Modern Language Association) style. The APA, like the MLA, uses in-text documentation instead of the traditional footnotes, and requires an alphabetized list of references. The term "References" is used rather than the "Works Cited" as employed in the MLA style. The year of the research is inserted prominently in APA, but less so in MLA.

1. Put the year immediately after the authority's name:
   Seidman (1983) explains that the role of brain dysfunction has been suspected but unproven since Kraepelin (1919) and Bleuler (1950) described the syndrome first (p. 195).
2. If you do not cite the name of the authority, insert the name of the authority, year, and the page numbers in parentheses.
   One psychiatrist argues that the concept that the brain is pathologically involved in the schizophrenic process has been agreed upon recently by the identification of a wide spectrum of neurological and metabolic disorders (Seidman, 1983, pp. 195–196). Notice p. or pp. is used for pages in the APA system.
3. In a direct short quotation or a paraphrase found on a specific page, include the author, year, and page number(s).
   The psychological researcher posits that "interest in discovering the neuropathology of the schizophrenias began shortly after Kraepelin (1919) delineated the syndrome of dementia praecox" (Seidman, 1983, p. 196). APA requires the p. for page.
4. A long quotation (more than four lines of typing on the rough draft) is set off from the text in a block with no quotation marks needed as is followed in the MLA.
   Humphreys and Revelle (1984) find:

Indent 5 spaces for long quotation, not ten as in MLA.

> There are two major approaches to the study of human intellectual performance. The first focuses on the effect of personality and individual differences, and the second attempts to develop general laws of cognitive psychology or information processing. Although these two approaches rarely are combined, it is difficult to find an example of cognitive performance that is not better understood by a combination of both areas (p. 153).

← APA long quotation is double spaced like that of MLA.

5. For two authors, used both names: (Trimble and Kingsley, 1978). For three authors, name them all in the first entry: Dunlap, (1928), Rowland and Mettler, (1949) and then refer to them as Dunlap et al. (1928, 1949). For four or more authors, employ: Tatetsu et al. (1964).
6. Use the term "References" instead of "Works Cited" for the APA bibliography. Alphabetize the list of references at the end of the research paper. List chronologically two or more works by the same author: Kraepelin's 1919 work would precede Kraepelin's 1921 research. PARTS FOR AN ENTRY FOR A BOOK ARE: name(s) of author(s); date within parentheses; title of book underlined with only first word capitalized; city of publication, not abbreviated; and the name of the publisher.

EXAMPLE OF BOOK IN REFERENCES, APA

For example:

Edinger, E. F. (1972). Ego and archetype: Individuation and the religious function of the psyche. New York: Putnam's.

7. PARTS FOR AN ENTRY FOR A PERIODICAL (JOURNAL OR MAGAZINE) ARTICLE ARE: name(s) of the author(s); date within parentheses; title of article without quotation marks and with ONLY THE FIRST WORD CAPITALIZED; name of the journal underlined with all major words capitalized; volume number underlined, and inclusive page numbers.

EXAMPLE OF ARTICLE IN REFERENCES, APA

Humphreys, M. S. and Revelle, W. (1984). Personality, motivation, and performance: A Theory of the relationship between individual differences and information processing. Psychological Review, 91, 153–184.

notice the use of the comma; no pp. for pages needed when volume number is used

Seidman, L. J. (1983). Schizophrenia and brain dysfunction: An Integration of recent neurodiagnostic findings. Psychological Bulletin, 94 (2) 195–238. No comma is used between volume and number when both are included

Notice that the pp. for pages used in the text itself for citation purposes is not needed in periodical references when the volume number is cited. If no volume, then p. or pp. is used.

MLA Style

Works Cited

Thomas, Lewis. The Lives of a Cell: Notes of a Biology Watcher. New York: Viking, 1974.
---. The Medusa and the Snail: More Notes of a Biology Watcher. New York: Viking, 1979.

APA Style

If you use more than one book or article by the same author, list the works in order of the publication date, earliest first. Repeat the author's name for each entry. The first line of each entry is flush with the left margin, and the following lines are indented five spaces.

References

Thomas, L. (1974). The Lives of a cell: Notes of a biology watcher. New York: Viking.
Thomas, L. (1979). The Medusa and the snail: More notes of a biology watcher. New York: Viking.

A STUDENT RESEARCH PAPER

This paper has been prepared according to the Publication Manual of the American Psychological Association (APA) Third Edition, 1983:

Cover sheet is not numbered.

School Phobia: Causes, Symptoms, and Treatment

Title is caps and lower case

by

Patrice Kerins

Psychology 212, Section 01

Honors

Dr. J. Matthew Pirone

Spring, 1986

This paper has been prepared according to the

Publication Manual of the American Psychological

Association (APA) Third Edition, 1983

Always identify which format and style you are following, either MLA or APA.

Method: Analysis

Topic Outline

OUTLINE

School Phobia: Causes, Symptoms, and Treatment

Thesis: To reveal the world of the school phobia in analyzing this disputed and mysterious psychological problem of children. To explore further explanations and definitions of this phobia, its causes, symptoms, and methods of treatment.

I. INTRODUCTION

A. Purpose of school

B. Importance of attendance

C. Four reasons for absenteeism
1. Illness
2. Parental withdrawal
3. Truancy
4. School phobia

Thesis is stated here at the end of the introduction

II. BODY

A. Understanding and definition of school phobia

B. Separation anxiety: another definition of school phobia

C. Three popular theories on development of school phobia
1. Freudian
2. Cognitive
3. Behaviorist

D. Causes
1. At school
2. At home
a. Divorce
b. Separation
c. Arguments
d. Death
e. Economic problems
f. A new baby
g. Parents of school phobics (possible mental disorders)
h. Family size
i. Family order

E. Five Personality Features of School Phobics
   1. Anxiety
   2. Willfulness towards parents
   3. Dependence on parents
   4. Depression
   5. Unrealistic self-image

F. Symptoms
   1. Fictitious physical ailment
   2. Violence
   3. Refusal to work

G. Treatment
   1. Psychotherapy: Freudian theory
   2. Play therapy: cognitive theory
   3. Behaviorist therapy: classical and operant conditioning
   4. Other treatments

III. CONCLUSION

A. Return to thesis
B. Summary

Title page is not numbered.

School Phobia: Causes, Symptoms, and Treatment

short quotation

paraphrase

"Going to school is part of growing up in Western Society. The path leading from relatively dependent, protected state of childhood, to the state of responsible independence that characterizes the adult that goes through the school building" (Waller and Eisenberg, 1980, p. 209). In the preceding quotation Waller and Eisenberg (1980), two authorities on school psychiatry, explain the purpose of school and the importance of attendance. They further contend that school is important because one day children will have to support themselves, and school may be detrimental to a child's school development outside the family structure (1980, p. 209).

p. or pp is used for page or pages

paraphrase

If school is so important to a child's emotional growth, why are so many children absent from school each day? According to Maurice Tyerman (1968), there are four basic reasons why children are absent from school. The first reason is due to illness with parental permission. This cause affects about ninety percent of all absences. Second, parental withdrawal involves the parents' withdrawal of their children from school for their own purposes. Third, is truancy, when children do not go to school without parental permission. The fourth reason affects seventeen children out of one thousand. This phenomenon is known as school phobia (1980, p. 9).

thesis

The focus of this paper is to reveal the world of school phobia, analyzing this disputed and mysterious psychological problem of children. It will explore further explorations and definitions of this phobia, the phobia's causes, symptoms, and methods of treatment in order to fully understand school phobia.

short quotation

paraphrase

To study school phobia there must be an understanding of the term "phobia." "Phobia" is a persistent, excessive, unreasonable fear of a specific object, activity, or situation that results in a compelling desire to avoid the dreaded object, activity, or situation" (Goodwin, 1980, p. 24). Furthermore, Frank Falkner (1966) explains why phobias occur in children. He states that phobias in children are anxiety over physical harm or violating the standard code. Children develop phobias because they fear that there will be punishment from society if they do not live up to that standard code (p. 353).

student's own words, based on research

The development of phobias is usually not harmful or does not disable a person. Once a phobia is harmful to a person's life it becomes a deep-seated neurosis. School phobia is neurotic fear of school. Campbell (1981) gives a more formal definition: "School phobia--a school refusal syndrome, inability to attend school on a regular five-day basis because of pervasive anxiety and dramatic complaints" (p. 468). School phobia which is more prevalent among girls than boys, occurs in all economic classes, and peaks at the age of eleven or twelve (Goodwin, 1983, p. 69). A more indepth understanding of school phobia was given by G. Pollitt (1984):

Indent 5 spaces not 10 as for MLA

long quotation

> School phobia is a symptom of a variety of psychopathologies in childhood and adolescence. It may often be traced to the early interactions between infant and mother, and this phobic reaction is a manifestation of the failure to complete the separation--individualization process, school phobia is a symptom of separation anxiety that is often displaced on the school by children with an identity problem. (pp. 89-90)

Period before parenthesis

Pollitt makes clear that school phobia is separation anxiety and usually is between mother and child.

paraphrase

There is a dispute over the labeling and using the term "school phobia." The reason is that it is a separation anxiety which can be caused by other factors besides the person's own self. The causes of this phobia are considered unreasonable fears. In most cases the child is not afraid of school but is avoiding leaving home (Balter, 1985, p. 114). Professor J. Matthew Pirone suggests that to be a phobic is to be a shell of a person--hollow and fragmented. But we know with school phobics that the fault is not necessarily an attitude influenced by the school (Lecture, 1986). A psychology reference book as well does not consider this fear of school as school phobia. This source classifies it as a separation-anxiety (Oltmanns, Neale, Davidson, 1983, p. 299). These authorities believe that the term "school phobia" is being misused. They are concerned that a misrepresentation of this neurosis will cause people not to take it into account (p. 299).

paraphrases

students' own words

There are many different theories and hypotheses on the development of school phobia. The three most popular theories are the Freudian Theory, Cognitive Theory, and Behaviorist Theory.

Freudians believe that phobias, such as school phobia are developed by ". . . a defense against, the anxiety produced by id impulses. The anxiety linked to a particular id impulse is said to be displaced to an object or situation that has some symbolic connection to the impulse" (Oltmanns, Neale, Davidson, 1985, p. 299). School phobia from a Freudian point of view would consider the id impulse as a child's desire to be with the parent. Knowing this fact is impossible at school, the child develops a phobic reaction to school which is caused by the child's repressed impulse.

The Cognitive Theory concerning school phobia is developed by a malfunction in a child's sensory and motor skills which distorts a child's concept of space. The child's misconception of abstract space causes him or her to conceive people or objects, that are removed from their special environment, to appear much further off than they are in all actuality. This causes problems

short quotation and paraphrase

in a child's spacial relationships (familiar environment and people) which result in a separation anxiety like school phobia (Bauer, 1980, p. 192).

paraphrase

Behaviorists developed three hypotheses according to Oltmanns, Neale, and Davidson (1983). First, ". . . certain kinds of neutral stimuli are more likely than others to be conditioned to fear" (p. 300). Second, ". . . phobic reaction can be learned by imitating others" (p. 301). "A third behavioral hypothesis concerns operant conditioning. Perhaps phobic avoidance is directly rewarded. For whatever reason the child begins to shy away from school; this behavior is reinforced by the parents" (p. 301).

short quotations

The preceding three theories give a clear view of how school phobia develops in children. The question now is what are the actual causes of school phobia?

Most authorities agree that the underlying factors are home or school related. In most cases it is related to the home.

students' own words

The factors at school which may develop a phobic reaction are an intimidating teacher, gym class (undressing in front of others), class participation, toilet phobias, a "bully", or appearance (Goodwin, 1980, p. 69). Factors related to school which cause school phobias are usually resolved quickly. The more serious cases of school phobia are due to the home. Again, Prof. Pirone explains: "And perhaps the reactions to school aren't the essence of the problem.

short quotation and paraphrase

Perhaps attitudes to school stem from feelings which are unrelated to the educational framework" (Lecture, 1986). The root is the child's home, perhaps.

Goodwin (1980), states that primary causes of school phobia are due to divorce, separation, arguing within the home, death, economical problems or a new baby in the house (pp. 70-71). There was one study done in Japan on school phobic children. The results concluded that with the breakdown of the traditional family the children had a difficult time coping with the increased competition of the schools (Wakabayshi, 1982, pp. 160-180).

paraphrase

The family members and structure are probably major aspects in the causes of school phobia. The agreement among most authorities is that parents of school phobics usually have their own mental disorders. The parents are usually over protective, have an unsuccessful relationship between one another, and may have the same separation anxiety as the child (Waller and Eisenberg, 1980, p. 223).

In most cases it is the mother who has the mental disorder since she has long been appointed in Western culture to be in charge of childcare. Freehill (1973) discusses in his book, Disturbed and Troubled Children that school phobia can be caused by a mother's emotional problems. He declares "A mother, motivated because she is unable to give generous love, becomes overprotective and communicates anxiety about the child's welfare" (p. 106). He further argues that school phobia is due to

short quotation and paraphrase

a mother's inability to love. They continue to say that school phobia is a child's defense mechanism for hostility which is caused by lack of love (p. 107).

According to Ian Berg (1980), other factors are family size and family order. He reported that the older aged mother and youngest child usually causes dependency, as well as, over protectiveness, which causes school phobia (p. 239). Common sense indicates to one that not all cases of school phobia are due to all the causes mentioned. For instance, not all school phobics have emotionally disturbed parents or intimidating teachers. The causes of school phobia can become very complicated and vary from case to case.

How does one detect his or her child is school phobic? There are five personality features of a school phobic summarized by Jerome Wont (1983). The first is anxiety and the second is willfulness toward parents. The third is dependency on the parents. The fourth and fifth are depression and unrealistic self image (pp. 27-32). These personality traits combined with symptoms diagnose a school phobic.

paraphrase

The first symptom of school phobia is a fictitious physical ailment. The child will complain of not feeling well. The child convinces the parents to keep him or her home. The child recovers from illness after being told he or she does not have to go to school (Goodwin, 1983, p. 69).

If a school phobic is forced to go to school, the

symptoms become worse. Robert Golderson (1970) summarizes the symptoms that can occur:

Indent 5 spaces here, not 10 as in MLA

> If the older children are forced to go to school, they may become violent, refuse to do any work or participate in any activity. The younger child reacts by becoming frightened, tense, apprehensive, and by crying convulsively and trying to run out. (p. 1173)

long quotation

According to Jules and Zelda Segal (1986) school phobics will also show signs of anxiety, not only going to school, but whenever separated from the family. The child will have an anxiety reaction if he or she goes to a relatives or neighbors home and possibly when going to play with friends (p. 152).

So how does one treat school phobia? Authorities agree the quicker the school phobia is back to school the less detrimental it will be to the child's development. Mary D'Amico (1985) makes a statement agreeing with this conclusion. ". . . that the longer the child is allowed to remain at home the more uncomfortable he or she will feel about being separated from the parents and he or she will fall behind both academically and socially" (p. 87).

Importantly, psychotherapy is one method of treatment based on Freudian Theory. The psychotherapist's approach is to interview each family member alone and then as a group. The objective of the

short quotations and paraphrase

therapist is to find the behavior within the family that is causing this anxiety in the child (Lewis, 1980, p. 253). "Specifically, the families of children who refuse to attend school have dependency needs that are unmet, aggression that is poorly dealt with and an approach to relief in which each family member continuously seeks gratification but experiences disappointment and anger in relation to other members" (Lewis, 1980, p. 253). The therapist does analyze each family members' conscious and unconscious to uncover the pathological problem within the family. At this point, the therapist will begin to work with the child to relieve the hostility and aggression the child feels. The therapist will also work with the family to counsel them how to meet these unmet needs (Lewis, 1980, p. 254).

Another method is play therapy which is based on Cognitive Theory because it views the child from its own environment and does intimidate the child (Oltmanns, Neale, Davidson, 1985, p. 299). The therapist will analyze the child from a play therapy room. "A play therapy room is equipped with toys such as puppets, puzzles, sand and water, and rubber clowns. The child might be asked to arrange little dolls to represent dinnertime home" (Oltmanns, Neale, Davidson, 1985, pp. 299-300). The therapist will then analyze the child's representation of home and find what is causing this separation-anxiety (Oltmanns, Neale, Davidson, 1985, p. 300).

short quotations and paraphrase

The Behaviorist treatment of school phobia uses classical and operant conditioning. Classical conditioning is used when the child is neurotic. Operant conditioning is used when a child suffers a mild case of school phobia (Freehill, 1973, p. 107). Barker states:

3 spaces

> The Behavior therapist takes the view that such problem behaviors are learned, usually mainly through the child's experiences at home, and can be eliminated and replaced by other behaviors through the provision of new learning experiences. He therefore seeks to bring about appropriate changes in the child's environment and may often prefer to locate the treatment in the environment itself (236).

long quotation

3 spaces

Certainly, the Behaviorist treatment is the most popular of the three theories, and it also has proved to be quite effective in most instances.

student's own words

The three treatments mentioned above are the basis for many other treatments, such as the desensitization therapy, peer counseling therapy, and the therapeutic milieu. And certainly other treatments are still being explored. It should be stressed that treatment is a necessity in most cases. For if school phobia is not taken care of, that is, treated early in a child's life, it can lead to many serious psychological problems (Pirone, Lecture, 1986).

students conclusion in the student's own words

After having explored the definitions, causes,

student's own words

symptoms, and treatments of school phobia as well as its seriousness, one realizes, again, the need for a child's acceptance must be accomplished within the family. It is in that environment that the foundation of a healthy personality is set. It is through the child's mother and father, and then his or her siblings, that the child seeks human contact and security. If a child has to start school without an inner sense of security and peace, he or she may indeed find school a frightening experience which often leads to school phobia.

Conclusion returns to thesis and goes somewhat beyond.

Bibliographic entries are called References

Notice: date follows author's name in parenthesis

References

Balter, L. (1985, October). Understanding kids. Ladies Home Journal, p. 114.

Barker, P. (1976). Basic child psychiatry. Baltimore: U Park P. (l.c. l.c. — only first word of book title is capitalized)

Bauer, D. (1980). Childhood fears in a development perspective. In Out of school. L. Hersov and I. Berg, (Eds.). London: Wiley. (titles of books are underlined)

Berg, I. (1980). School refusal in early adolescence. In Out of school. L. Hersov and I. Berg (Eds.). London: Wiley.

Campbell, J. (1981). Phobia, school. Psychiatric dictionary. New York: Oxford UP. (Month of periodical is added within parenthesis)

D'Amico, M. L. (1985, September). When kids won't go to school. McCalls, pp. 86-87. (pp. is abbreviation for pages.)

Diamond, S. C. (1985, November). School phobic adolescents and a peer support group. Clearing House, pp. 125-126.

Falkner, F. (Ed). (1966). Human development. Philadelphia: Saunders.

Freehill, M. (1973). Disturbed and troubled children. New York: Saunders.

Golderson, R. (1970). School phobia. The Encyclopedia of human behavior. Garden City, NY: Doubleday.

Notice the period after the parenthesis for date.

all entries are doubled spaced

Notice that for parts or chapters of books or titles of Articles no quotation marks are used.

In APA the author's last name is placed first, followed by INITIALS of first and middle names, NOT FULL NAMES

Goodwin, D. W. (1983). Phobia: The Facts. London: Oxford UP.

Hsia, H. (1984, July). Structural and strategic approach to school phobia. Psychology in the Schools, pp. 360-367. Rpt. from the Psychological Abstracts. 71 (11) 3125. ← No p. is used here because earlier volume (71) is cited.

Hersov, L. and Berg, I. (Eds.) (1980). Out of school. London: Wiley.

Hersov, L. (1980). Hospital treatment of school refusal. In Out of school. L. Hersov and I. Berg (Eds.). London: Wiley.

Kennedy, J. A. (1984, May). School phobia: When children are afraid of school, there are things parents can do to help. Parents, pp. 137-140.

Lewis, M. (1980). Psychotherapeutic treatment in school refusal. In Out of school. L. Hersov and I. Berg (Eds.). London: Wiley.

Oltmanns, T. and Neale, J. and Davidson, G. (1983). Case studies in abnormal psychology. New York: Wiley.

Pirone, Dr. J. M. (1986, April). Phobias. Lecture presented in Psychology 212, Honors, Rockland Community College, Suffern, NY, April 15, 1986.

Pollitt, G. (1984). School phobia. School Social Work Journal, pp. 80-90. Rpt. 1985 from Social Work Research and Abstracts, 21 (1), 110.

Segal, J. and Z. (1986, February). When your kids won't go to school. Parents, p. 152.

Titles of lectures have no quotation marks, nor do chapter titles or titles of articles.

When volume 21 is used, no p. is used for 110.

volume numbers are underlined; numbers are in parenthesis

Trueman, D. (1984, April). The Behavioral treatment of school phobia: A critical review. Psychology in the Schools, pp. 215-223. Rpt. from the Psychological Abstracts, 71 (8).

Tyerman, M. (1968). Truancy. London: U of London P.

Wakabayshi, S. (1982). The relationship between school refusal and social conditions in Japan. Japanese Journal of Child and Adolescent Psychiatry, pp. 160-180. Rpt. from the Psychological Abstracts, 1982, 70 (4).

Waller, D. and Eisenberg, L. (1980). School refusal in childhood--a psychiatric-pediatric perspective. In Out of school. L. Hersov and I. Berg (Eds.)

Wont, Jerome (1983). School-based intervention strategies for school phobia: A Ten-step common sense approach. Pointer, spring, pp. 27-32 Rpt. from the Psychological Abstracts, 1983, 71 (5).

Yale, W. and Hersov, L. and Treseder, J. Behavioral treatments of school refusal. In Out of school. L. Hersov and I. Berg (Eds). London: Wiley.

TENTH SESSION

Literary Research for Literature Students: A Student's Literary Research Paper (MLA)

1. Select a major literary writer.
2. If you have not read anything by the writer in question, you might wish to read a short story or a few poems by him or her. This reading should provide you with some of the ideas and style of the writer.
3. You have chosen to write your research paper on one aspect of the literature of D. H. Lawrence.
4. In the college library, look up the writer's last name: LAWRENCE, D. H., IN THE SUBJECT SIDE OF THE CARD CATALOGUE. Lawrence's name will be typed at the top of the subject card. Underneath Lawrence's name in commercial printing will be <u>the title of a book about Lawrence</u>, that is, <u>a secondary source</u> on Lawrence. (Lawrence himself is the subject of this book.)
   (All the books written by D. H. Lawrence can be located in the card catalogue IN THE AUTHOR-TITLE SIDE OF THE CARD CATALOGUE. All the books by Lawrence are considered <u>primary sources</u>.) <u>Secondary sources</u> may also be found in periodicals, reviews, literary magazines, and newspapers. See <u>Social Science and Humanities Index</u>, the <u>New York Times Index</u>, the <u>Essay and General Literature Index</u>. See also REFERENCE BOOKS on Literature—PN through PZ in the Reference Section. See examples further on in these instructions.
5. By reading secondary sources in both books and periodicals, you will discover some idea that may interest you as a possible thesis for your paper on Lawrence. For example, many secondary sources interpret an Oedipal relationship in Lawrence's novels.
6. You decide on the thesis of the Oedipal Pattern in <u>Sons and Lovers</u>, a major Lawrence novel. You select this idea because it occurred to you during an earlier reading of <u>Sons and Lovers</u>, and also it was mentioned in some of the secondary sources you consulted. YOU MUST ESTABLISH YOUR THESIS BY FINDING SECONDARY SOURCES BY LITERARY CRITICS WHICH DEAL WITH THE OEDIPAL PATTERN IN <u>SONS AND LOVERS</u>. THESE SECONDARY SOURCES CAN ALSO BE USED TO SUPPORT THIS THESIS THROUGHOUT THIS PAPER. <u>MAKE NOTE CARDS ON THESE SECONDARY SOURCES INVOLVING THE OEDIPAL IDEA</u>.
7. Once you have established the thesis, and keeping it in mind, read <u>Sons and Lovers</u> again, if you have already read it once. Mark the passages in <u>Sons and Lovers</u> which suggest an Oedipal relationship. <u>MAKE NOTE CARDS ON THESE SECTIONS</u>. DEVELOP THE PAPER AROUND THIS THESIS, BOTH IN TERMS OF USING WHATEVER SECONDARY SOURCES YOU HAVE DISCOVERED AS WELL AS INCLUDING SHORT QUOTATIONS AND PARAPHRASE FROM THE NOVEL, <u>SONS AND LOVERS</u>, WHICH IS THE PRIMARY SOURCE.

8. Although secondary sources are important to assist you to establish the thesis of the paper, the emphasis in the paper should be on the primary source, that is, the quotations and paraphrase from Sons and Lovers and some of your own reactions to Sons and Lovers. Some of your own reactions can be most effective in a literary research paper, YOU ARE PROVING THE THESIS BY DEMONSTRATING THAT YOU UNDERSTAND HOW LAWRENCE HAS INCORPORATED THAT OEDIPAL PATTERN IN SONS AND LOVERS, THAT IS, HOW LAWRENCE HAS INCORPORATED THE OEDIPAL PATTERN IN HIS PRIMARY SOURCE. USING ONLY SECONDARY SOURCES BY CRITICS RE: THE OEDIPAL PATTERN IN SONS AND LOVERS MAKES AN INEFFECTUAL PAPER. See literature paper on War and Peace in the last part of the Guide.

NOTE: Using only secondary sources in a literature paper which involves the analysis of one or more primary sources, such as Sons and Lovers, is unacceptable.

A STUDENT RESEARCH PAPER

This paper has been prepared according to the Modern Language Association (MLA) Handbook for Writing Research Papers published in July 1984.

Cover sheet is not numbered.

War and Peace:

Tolstoy's Views on Women--

Archetypal and Personal

title is caps and lower case

by

Kimberly Pfaff

English 220, Section 01, Honors

Professor Samuel Draper

Fall 1986

This paper has been prepared according to the new Modern Language Association (MLA) Style Sheet Published in July 1984

Always identify which format and style you are following in your research paper, either MLA or APA.

Method: Cause and Effect and Analysis

Topic Outline

OUTLINE

War and Peace: Tolstoy's Views on Women: Archetypal and Personal

Thesis: (EFFECT) Tolstoy's views of women in War and Peace were archetypal and personal.

The paper will examine the Earth-Mother and the Femme Fatale archetypes in War and Peace, represented by Princess Maria Bolkonsky and Ellen Kuragin, and their correlation to Tolstoy's own disparate views of women.

I. INTRODUCTION

- A. Novel: representation of author's experience and views
- B. War and Peace
  1. Heroic epic
  2. Philosophic work
  3. Bildungsroman
  4. Archetypal approach: Earth-Mother and Femme Fatale

II. BODY

- A. Definition of Earth-Mother archetype
- B. Definition of Femme Fatale archetype
- C. Princess Maria as Earth-Mother
  1. Psychologically and religiously
  2. Physically
- D. Ellen Kuragin as Femme Fatale
  1. Physically
  2. Psychologically
  3. Male victims of Femme Fatale
     - a. Youthful
     - b. Passive and obscure

E. Examples of the two archetypes, Princess Maria and Ellen Kuragin in War and Peace

F. Tolstoy's personal views of women
   1. Angel: significance of chaste woman
      a. Savior of the world
      b. Bodiless and deprived of passions
      c. Chastity and Christian ideals: self-effacement and asceticism
   2. Devil
      a. Beauty in women: a curse
      b. Morally inferior

G. Tolstoy himself a misanthrope and misogynist

III. CONCLUSION

A. Maria and Ellen: polarities held by Tolstoy
B. All women: predators except for those chaste, religious, and subservient
C. Dichotomization: looking glass into Tolstoy's soul

Title page is not numbered.

War and Peace:
Tolstoy's View on Women:
Archetypal and Personal

A novel is more than an elaborately planned set of characters and events; it is the innermost feelings, perceptions, and reflections of one individual set down in written form. Though the people and places may be varied and far away, they nonetheless are taken from the author's own life and represent his personal experiences and views.

This is especially true of War and Peace (1869) by Leo Tolstoy (1828-1910). Hailed as an heroic epic, a philosophic work, and a bildungsroman, or novel of education, it also provides, through the use of archetypes, an insightful glimpse into Tolstoy's estimation of the female sex. This paper, then, will examine the Earth-Mother and Femme Fatale archetypes in War and Peace, represented by Princess Maria Bolkonsky and Ellen Kuragin, and their correlation to Tolstoy's own disparate views of women.

The Earth-Mother, as Oliver Evans and Harry Finestone assert in The World of the Short Story: Archetypes in Action is "the personification of nature or the creative source" (57). As such, she is characterized by her ability to nourish, sustain, and

students' own words

use birth and death dates of major figures

thesis

short quotation and paraphrase

use dates in parenthesis for all primary sources

quotations and paraphrase from secondary sources

notice the period goes after the parenthesis ( ).

endure (57). These authorities further suggest that "the omnipresence of an earth goddess in the mythologies of the world is proof of the universality of the Mother Archetype" (57). Evans and Finestone also find Earth-Mother self-sacrificing and forebearing (58).

The Femme Fatale, on the other hand, is strikingly different. Beautiful in a traditionally pale fashion, Evans and Finestone reveal that she is methodically destructive--choosing passive men as her victims to mercilessly torture them physically and/or emotionally. She is cold and unfeeling, determined to attain all her desires--at the peril of all who stand in her way (19).

Throughout War and Peace, Princess Maria emerges clearly as the long-suffering, comforting Earth-Mother. Resembling, according to family friends, Tolstoy's own mother, Princess Marie Volkonsky (Ellis 180) possesses the altruistic, forgiving nature characteristic of the archetype: "My vocation is to be happy in the happiness of others, in the happiness of love and self-sacrifice" (WP 210). Ruth Crego Benson, a literary critic, labels Maria "a self-effacing, ascetic woman, who lacks completely the sexual dimension" (66) that is so vital a part of Ellen's being. Indeed, Maria repeatedly confirms her preference for the divine, sublime love over more earthy passion: ". . . Christian love, the love of our neighbor . . . is sweeter than those feelings that may be inspired in a poetic, loving

paraphrase

quotations from secondary sources

quotation from primary source War and Peace

young girl . . . . by the fine eyes of a young man (WP 81). Throughout her life, she yearns for nothing more than "another happiness unattainable in this life" (WP 1076).

Physically, Maria is not particularly pleasing to look at; though much is made of her bright, shining eyes, she is far from attractive: "The poor girl is devilishly ugly" (WP 204), Anatole thinks upon first seeing her. Even her father makes no pretense concerning her appearance: "She has no need to disfigure herself--she's ugly enough without that" (WP 203).

What Maria lacks in outward beauty, though, is more than compensated for by her inner goodness and unwavering spirituality: "[Maria] vowed to . . . . love . . . . all her fellow-creatures, as Christ loved men. Countess Marya's soul was always striving towards the infinite, the external, and the perfect. . . ." (WP 1096). Her fine-tuned intuitiveness does not escape notice: "Marie, how she is wonderful!" [Natasha] said. "The insight she has into children. She seems to see straight into their souls" (WP 1097). In the end, her superior blend of intense faith and goodness proves a suitable enticement for Nikolay, and Maria fills up the one void in her life by marrying a man who truly loves and appreciates her: "The very groundwork of his steady and tender love and pride in his wife was always this feeling of awe at her spirituality, at that elevated moral world that he could hardly enter, in which his wife always

Notice how student demonstrates the thesis by quoting War and Peace, the primary source.

abbreviate titles of primary sources after full title is used in the text.

students own words and short quotations from primary source War and Peace.

A formal introduction with colon:

4

lived" (WP 1094). *introduces the long quotation*

Ellen Kuragin, by contrast, as the novel's Femme Fatale, is Maria's exact opposite. In the tradition of the archetype she symbolizes, Ellen is exquisite:

Notice 3 spaces before... *Triple spacing*

> Princess Ellen smiled. She got up with the same unchanging smile of the acknowledged beauty with which she had entered the drawing-room. Her white ball-dress adorned with ivy and moss rustled lightly; her white shoulders, glossy hair, and diamonds glittered, as she passed between the men who moved apart to make way for her. Not looking directly at any one, but smiling at every one, as it were courteously allowing to all the right to admire the beauty of her figure, her full shoulders, her bosom and back . . . she moved up to Anna Pavlovna, seeming to bring with her the brilliance of the ballroom. (WP 8)

long quotation is indented 10 spaces left margin

and after long quotation *Triple spacing*

However, as Ruth Davies warns in The Great Books of Russia, "her beautifully chiselled face is a mask from Hell" (WP 268). To help convey her treacherous nature, Tolstoy employs cold, hard adjectives to describe her: her skin is like "marble" (WP 11), her shoulders "statuesque" (WP 12). As a traditional Femme Fatale, her beauty is pale and bloodless, as denoted by the "cold, alabastrine magnificence of [her] shoulders" (WP 12).

Here, more than three lines or spaces have been left before and after the long quotation, but in your paper only three spaces are used.

Certainly, these phrases serve to further illustrate her icily fatal nature.

Indeed, Ellen is deceptively destructive; her intoxicating beauty is but a thin veil sheathing, as Davies states, the "basilisk" within (266). Preying upon men for her sport, she unerringly chooses those over whom she holds control. Mario Praz asserts in his The Romantic Agony, as reported in Archetypes in Action, that the male victim of the Femme Fatale usually lacks an aggressive nature:

Triple spacing

long quotation from secondary source.

> The lover is usually a youth, and maintains a passive attitude; he is obscure, and inferior either in condition or in physical exuberance to the woman, who stands in the same relation to him as do the female spiders, the praying mantis, etc., to their respective males: sexual cannibalism is her monopoly. (Praz in Evans and Finestone 20)

Triple spacing

Certainly, this passage fully describes Pierre and Ellen's relationship, which is not, of course, based on mutual friendship or love. Indeed, from the very start Pierre senses danger: "There is something nasty in the feeling she excites in me, something not legitimate" (WP 187). His instinct warns him there is "something vile and unnatural in this marriage" (WP 187). Yet he sees

Ellen in "all her womanly beauty" (<u>WP</u> 188), and is totally overcome: "Already she had power over him" (<u>WP</u> 186). Throughout the entire affair, Pierre is rendered helpless, swept away to take part in a marriage in his very soul assures him is wrong:

3 spaces before

> "So you have never noticed till now that I am lovely?" Ellen seemed to be saying. "You haven't noticed that I am a woman? Yes, I am a woman, who might belong to any one--to you, too," her eyes said. And at that moment Pierre felt that Ellen not only could, but would become his wife, that it must be so.
>
> He knew it at that moment as surely as he would have known it, standing under the wedding crown beside her. How would it be? and when? He knew not, knew not even if it would be a good thing (he had a feeling, indeed, that for some reason it would not), but he knew it would be so. (<u>WP</u> 186)

and 3 spaces after the long quotation.

Unlike Maria, Ellen oozes with sexuality, and is openly aggressive in attaining all she desires:

3 spaces

> He would have bent over her hand and have kissed it. But with an almost brutal movement of her head, she caught at his lips and pressed them to

Owing to technical makeup problems, more than three spaces were left before and after the long quotation; however, in your paper you should use only three spaces.

quotations from <u>War and Peace</u>, the primary source.

her own. Pierre was struck by the transformed, the unpleasantly confused expression on her face. (WP 193)

3 spaces

Like a viper, she ruthlessly strikes her victims, leaving them helpless in the wake of her venomous beauty. She is a depraved woman, stripped of conscience and morality; only her own self-interest matters. As Pierre later reflects, after their marriage has fallen to pieces: "The solution of the whole riddle lay in that fearful word, that she is a dissolute woman; I have found that fearful word, and all has become clear" (WP 289).

In creating Maria and Ellen, Tolstoy brings to life what Benson terms his "icons of woman--as angel and as devil" (10). Maria's purity of soul--and body--is an ideal in Tolstoy's eyes: "Oh, how I would like to show to women all the significance of a chaste woman. A chaste woman . . . will save the world" (Tolstoy in Benson 10). Vladimir Chertkov, the author's friend and disciple, affirms Maria's importance: "[Tolstoy] absolutely discriminated in favor of the intelligent, religious woman whom he seldom happened to meet in life" (Chertkov 11). And certainly, as Davies observes, there is no doubt that Tolstoy lavished upon her utter devotion as an author (234). For, as Benson attests, his "'best' women . . . are bodiless, deprived of all passions save those directed toward family, chastity, or the

student's own reaction in her own words

quotations and paraphrase from secondary sources on Tolstoy

Christian ideals of self-effacement and asceticism" (11).

Ellen, however, holds a different place in Tolstoy's heart, representing the egocentric, erotic creature he finds so threatening to men, and upon which he thrusts, as fellow author Maxim Gorky observes, his "implacable hostility" (Gorky in Benson 9):

3 spaces

long quotation

> Regard the society of women as an inevitable evil of social life, and avoid them as much as possible. Because from whom do we actually learn voluptuousness, effeminacy, frivolity in everything and a multitude of other vices, if not from women? Who is responsible for the fact that we lose such feelings inherent in us as courage, firmness, prudence, equity, and so on, if not women? (Tolstoy in Benson 9)

3 spaces

For Tolstoy, a woman's beauty is not a blessing, but a curse; it is a tool which she skillfully uses to her every advantage, at the expense of those around her. In his eyes, the more attractive a woman is, the more she deceives: "A beautiful woman smiles, and we think that because she smiles she is expressing something good and true. But often the smile means something entirely foul" (Tolstoy in Benson 10). Certainly, Benson posits, it is this hardline stance which leads him to declare that woman is, "in all respects, morally [man's] inferior" (Tolstoy in Benson 9). In Ellen, then, Tolstoy creates the embodiment of all he distrusts and despises in women, confirming, as Renato Poggioli asserts in *The Phoenix and the Spider*, that he was "not only, like Alceste, a misanthrope: unlike him, he was a misogynist too" (70).

Maria and Ellen, finally representing the *Earth-Mother* and *Femme Fatale* archetypes in *War and Peace*, are prime examples of the polarity with which Tolstoy views women. He sees no fine line, no subtle shading between "good" and "bad": all women are treacherous predators, save those who are meekly chaste and subservient--more succinctly, save those who are neutered of their own sexuality. Thus, his dichotomization throughout the novel reflects more than just the opposite traits of two fictional characters; like a looking-glass, it provides a mirror into Tolstoy's very soul.

Conclusion returns to the thesis

students' own words conclude the paper

Bibliographic entries are called Works Cited.

Notice abbreviations and shortened forms of publishers' names.

lower case ed. is required with this usage.

Works Cited

Titles of books are underlined.

Benson, Ruth Crego. Women in Tolstoy: The Ideal and the Erotic. Urbana: U of Illinois P, 1973.

Chertkov, Vladimir. The Journal of Leo Tolstoy 1895-1899. New York: Vintage, 1917.

Davies, Ruth. The Great Books of Russia. Norman: U of Oklahoma P, 1968.

Ellis, Havelock. The New Spirit. New York: Kraus, 1969.

Evans, Oliver and Harry Finestone, eds. The World of the Short Story: Archetypes in Action. New York: Knopf, 1971.

Gorky, Maxim. Lev Tolstoj. Sobranie socineni ja. In Women in Tolstoy. By Ruth Crego Benson.

Poggioli, Renato. The Phoenix and the Spider. Cambridge: Harvard UP, 1956.

Praz, Mario. "The Romantic Agony." In Archetypes in Action Eds. Oliver Evans and Harry Finestone.

Tolstoy, Leo. Polnoe sobranie socinenij. In Women in Tolstoy. By Ruth Crego Benson.

Tolstoy, Leo. War and Peace. New York: Modern, n.d.

Capital Ed. is required in this usage.

Titles of articles or sections (chapters) are put in quotation marks.

No date given for this edition

Note that p. for page is not used in MLA, nor is pp. for pages.

all entries are double spaced.

INDEX